A
Marty Haugen
Songbook

Pauline
2011

Decani Music

Published by Decani Music, Oak House, 70 High Street, Brandon, Suffolk, IP27 0AU
http://www.decanimusic.co.uk

Cover illustrations by permission of GIA Publications, Inc. 7404 S.Mason Ave, Chicago. IL 60638.
http://www.giamusic.com/

ISBN 978-1-900314-18-3

Printed by Quadrant, Riverside House, Dicker Mill, Hertford, SG13 7AE

Foreword

FROM ITS BIRTH AND DOWN THROUGH THE SUCCEEDING CENTURIES until today, Christian worship has embraced and incorporated a wonderfully rich and diverse mélange of music and languages to give every community in every culture a voice to express their praise, remembrance and petition. I believe this richness and diversity is an essential means for God's voice to sing to and through us.

For that reason, I was somewhat uncomfortable with the idea of a 'songbook' that was mainly limited to my own compositions. A number of years ago, at the first liturgical gathering of Australian Roman Catholics in Melbourne, the Rev. John Bell of the Church of Scotland said to the gathered Australian musicians, 'You do not need to only sing the songs of North America. You have your own voice.'

Amen to that. The English-speaking churches of England, Wales, Scotland and Ireland have a long tradition of providing 'psalms, hymns and inspired songs' for their own congregations and to the wider church throughout the world. From Wesley and Watts to Brian Wren, Fred Pratt Green, Timothy Dudley-Smith, Bernadette Farrell, John Bell, Stephen Dean, Christopher Walker and Paul Inwood and many others, the English-speaking churches of Europe have offered the world a true, faithful and beautiful Christian repertoire.

Yet when Stephen Dean suggested creating this songbook I was humbled and grateful that a composer, parish musician, editor and publisher that I greatly respect would think that such a resource could be a helpful supplement to such a solid existing body of ritual song. I respect his liturgical judgment, his pastoral sensibilities and his selfless commitment to provide helpful support for Christian (and especially Roman Catholic) communities across the British Isles.

In those blessed times when I have been with English, Welsh, Scottish and Irish parish musicians, I have experienced in them a similar passionate and selfless commitment for their communities and its faithful worship. If these songs can in any way help them in their labours on behalf of God's children, it is a small repayment for the inspiration and hope they have given to me.

Soli Deo Gloria.

Marty Haugen

Introduction

Of the approximately 300 pieces by Marty Haugen in the GIA catalogue, this songbook contains only 85. It aims to be a representative selection of the many genres with which Marty has enriched the liturgy in the last thirty years.

As a Lutheran, Marty has been able to bring a distinctive view to the composition of music to serve the Catholic liturgy at a unique moment in its history. The time following the Second Vatican Council (1962-65) has been one of rapid liturgical development which, although affecting particularly the Roman Catholic church, has extended over all denominations. The revised Roman Missal and Lectionary created for Catholics an urgent need for music for the Mass in English. This music had to serve ritual needs of which Catholics had no previous experience, such as the Responsorial Psalm and processional songs for the Gathering and Communion to be sung by the whole congregation rather than a schola or choir. Marty Haugen's contribution to the development of this new repertoire has been extensive and irreplaceable.

But though this collection has been compiled with the liturgy in mind, Marty's output also includes a notable series of performance pieces, from *Tales of Wonder* and *Agape* through to the three Gospel-based musicals, *The Song of Mark*, *The Feast of Life* (Luke), and *That you may have life* (John). Some extracts from these works are represented here but their true flavour can only be appreciated by experiencing them in their entirety.

Another omission is Mass settings. At the time of compilation, Roman Catholics are awaiting a new translation of the Mass, which has not been approved for use. So one of Marty's most notable achievements, the Mass of Creation, has not been included. This is the reason for calling this volume A Songbook. A successor volume would be able to include eucharistic settings.

Other editions

Many of these pieces have been published in two forms: a simple form for hymnals, and extended choral arrangements (octavo editions.) In this book a compromise has been adopted for reasons of space; choral parts have been provided but do not include all the varied arrangements in the octavos. In particular, the changes of key at the end of the octavo arrangements have been omitted. In the copyright line of each song the octavo number has been provided as well as the name of the collection from which the music is taken. Octavos and complete collections can be ordered from Decani.

Topical index

The book is arranged in more or less chronological order, although the first place has been given to *Gather us in*, perhaps Marty Haugen's best-known song. This index will help find a song for a particular occasion.

Scriptural index, index of tunes, index of first lines: p 203

Gather Us In

Words and music by Marty Haugen

A C/G D/F♯ G A C/G
Gath-er us in— the lost and for-sak-en, Gath-er us in— the
Gath-er us in— the rich and the haugh-ty, Gath-er us in— the
Give us to drink the wine of com-pas-sion, Give us to eat the
Gath-er us in and hold us for ev-er, Gath-er us in and
D/F♯ G A D A C G
blind and the lame; Call to us now, and we shall a-wak-en,
proud and the strong; Give us a heart so meek and so low-ly,
bread that is you, Nou-rish us well, and teach us to fa-shion
make us your own; Gath-er us in— all peo-ples to-geth-er,
Gm/B♭ Dm C Am7 D C/D Gm6/D D
We shall a-rise at the sound of our name.
Give us the cour-age to en-ter the song.
Lives that are ho-ly and hearts that are true.
Fire of love in our flesh and our bone.

Eye has not seen

Refrain based on 1 Cor 2:9, 10

Words and music by Marty Haugen

Last time
teach us the wis - dom of God.
Last time
D/F♯ G D/A A7 G/D Last time D
Last time
Verses
1. When pain and sor - row weigh us down, be near to us, O
2. Our lives are but a sin - gle breath, we flow - er and we
3. To those who see with eyes of faith, the Lord is ev - er
4. We sing a mys - tery from the past in halls where saints have
C G/B Gm/B♭
Lord, for - give the weak - ness of our faith, and bear us up with-
fade, yet all our days are in your hands, so we re - turn in
near, re - flect - ed in the fac - es of all the poor and
trod, yet ev - er new the
1-3
D/A Bm7 D/F♯ C

D.C.
in your peace-ful word.
love what love has made.
low - ly of the world.
G/B D A G/A D/A A7
D.C.
4
mu - sic rings to Je - sus, Liv - ing Song of
D/F♯ C G/B
D.C.
God.
A G/A D/A A7
D.C.

We walk by faith

Henry Alford, 1810-71, alt.

SHANTI, CM
Marty Haugen

My soul in stillness waits

Vv. 1-4 based on the 'O' Antiphons
Vv. 5-6 by Marty Haugen

Marty Haugen

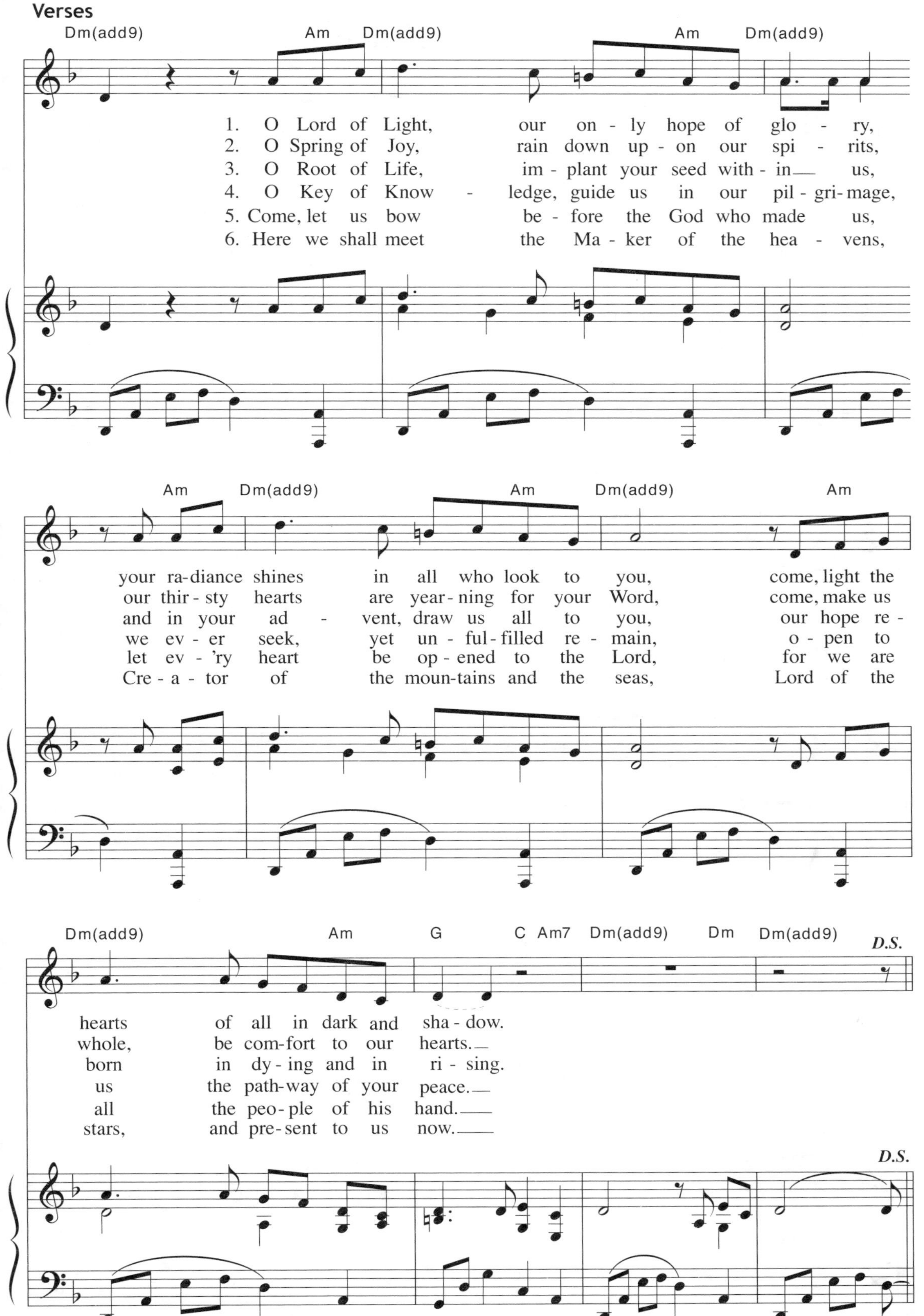
Verses
Dm(add9) Am Dm(add9) Am Dm(add9)
1. O Lord of Light, our on - ly hope of glo - ry,
2. O Spring of Joy, rain down up - on our spi - rits,
3. O Root of Life, im - plant your seed with - in us,
4. O Key of Know - ledge, guide us in our pil - gri - mage,
5. Come, let us bow be - fore the God who made us,
6. Here we shall meet the Ma - ker of the hea - vens,
Am Dm(add9) Am Dm(add9) Am
your ra - diance shines in all who look to you, come, light the
our thir - sty hearts are year - ning for your Word, come, make us
and in your ad - vent, draw us all to you, our hope re -
we ev - er seek, yet un - ful - filled re - main, o - pen to
let ev - 'ry heart be op - ened to the Lord, for we are
Cre - a - tor of the moun - tains and the seas, Lord of the
Dm(add9) Am G C Am7 Dm(add9) Dm Dm(add9)
D.S.
hearts of all in dark and sha - dow.
whole, be com - fort to our hearts.
born in dy - ing and in ri - sing.
us the path - way of your peace.
all the peo - ple of his hand.
stars, and pre - sent to us now.
D.S.

Rejoice, rejoice!

Words and music by Marty Haugen

UK agent Decani Music, Oak House, 70 High Street, Brandon IP27 0AU. **Octavo no:** G-2654 (GUI)

To you, O Lord

Psalm 25:4-5.8-9.10 R.v.1

Marty Haugen

 Octavo no: G-2653 (GUI/PsChY1)

Verses
mf
1. Lord, make me know your ways, teach me your
15
mp
2. For the Lord is good and right-eous, re veal-ing the
f
3. To the ones who seek the Lord, who look to God's
(Bm) Cm
(F#m/A) Gm/B♭
(Gmaj7) A♭maj7
(F#m7) Gm7
(Bm) Cm
paths, and keep me in the way of your truth, for you are
21
way to those who seek him,
G/D D♭/F
Word, who live God's love,
(Am7) B♭m7
(G) A♭
(D/F♯) E♭/G
(C/E) D♭/F
(G/D) A♭/E♭
(Cmaj7) D♭maj7

poco rit.
Response D.S.
2
God, my Sa - viour.
gent-ly lea-ding the
(Em7) (D/F♯) (G) (G/A) (A) (G/A) (A) (C/E) (G/D)
Fm7 E♭/G A♭ A♭/B♭ B♭ A♭/B♭ B♭ D♭/F A♭/E♭
Response D.S.
3
poor and the hum-ble.
God will al-ways be
(Em7) (D/F♯) (G) (G/A) (A) (G/A) (A) (C/E) (G/D)
Fm7 E♭/G A♭ A♭/B♭ B♭ A♭/B♭ B♭ D♭/F A♭/E♭
poco rit.
mp
poco rit.
Response D.S.
near, and will show them mer - cy.
(C) (G/B) (Em7) (D/F♯) (G) (G/A) (A) (G/A) (A)
D♭ A♭/C Fm7 E♭/G A♭ A♭/B♭ B♭ A♭/B♭ B♭
poco rit.

We Remember

Words and music by Marty Haugen

G
D/F♯
B7
Em
and we be lieve that we will see You when You come,
G7
C
(tacet)
G
Em
in your glo - ry, Lord we re - mem - ber,
ff
G/B
Am
Dsus4
G
C/D
we ce - le-brate, we be - lieve.
mf
G
C/D
To verses
Last time
G

Verses
G C/D G C/D
1. Here, a mil - lion woun-ded souls are year-ning just to touch You and be healed Ga - ther all Your peo - ple, and hold them to your heart.
2. Now, we re - cre - ate your love, we bring the bread and wine to share a meal Sign of grace and mer - cy, the pre - sence of the Lord.
3. Christ, the Fa-ther's great 'A - men,' to all the hopes and dreams of ev - 'ry heart Peace be - yond all tel - ling, and free - dom from all fear.
4. See the face of Christ re - vealed in ev - 'ry per - son stan-ding by your side Gift to one a - no - ther, and tem - ples of Your love.
G G/B C Em
Bm C A/C♯ D
D.S.
D.S.

Canticle of the Sun

Adapted from *Cantico di Frate Sole,* St Francis of Assisi
Refrain based on Psalm 19:1

Marty Haugen

 Octavo no: G-2788 (WOH)

sing to the
To verses
field, and sing, sing the glo - ry of the Lord.
(C) Eb
(F#m7) Am7
(E/G#) G/B
(A) C
(B) D
(E) G
(Esus 4) Gsus4
(E) G
Final
Lord.
Sing, sing to the glo - ry of the
(F#m7) Am7
(E/G#) G/B
(A) C
(B) D
(F#m7) Am7
(E/G#) G/B
(A) C
(B) D
fine
Lord.
(E) G
(Esus 4) Gsus4
(E) G
(Esus 4) Gsus4
(E) G
(Esus 4) Gsus4
(E) G
fine

1. Praise for the sun, the bring - er of day, He car - ries the light of the Lord in his rays; the moon and the stars who light up the way un - to your throne.
2. Praise for the wind that blows thro' the trees, the sea's migh - ty storms, the gen - tl - est breeze; they blow where they will, they blow where they please to please the Lord.
3. Praise for the rain that wa - ters our fields, and bless - es our crops so all the earth yields; from death un - to life her mys - tery re - vealed springs forth in joy.
4. Praise for the fire who gives us his light, the warmth of the sun to bright - en our night; he danc - es with joy, his spir - it so bright, he sings of you.
5. Praise for the earth who makes life to grow, the crea - tures you made to let your life show; the flow - ers and trees that help us to know the heart of love.
6. Praise for our death that makes our life real, the know - ledge of loss that helps us to feel; the gift of your - self, your pres - ence re - vealed to lead us home.
tacet
D.C.

We are many parts

Based on 1 Cor 12:13

Marty Haugen

 Octavo no: G-2917 (WOH)

May the Spi - rit of love make us one in - deed; one, the love that we share, one, our hope in des - pair, one, the cross that we bear.
(D) F
(D7) F7
(G) B♭
(Bb) D♭
(D) F
(G/D B♭/F
(D) F tacet
(Cadd 9) E♭add 9
Last time
(G/B) B♭/D
(Asus4) Csus 4 tacet
(D) F
(G/D) B♭/F
(D) F
(D/C♯) F/E
(D/B) F/D

Verses
1. God of all, we look to you,— we would be your ser - vants true, let us be your love to all the world.
2, So my pain is pain for you,— in your joy is my joy, too; all is brought to - geth - er in the Lord.
3. All you see - kers, great and small,- seek the grea - test gift of all; if you love, then you will know the Lord.
(A) C
(Em9/A) Gm9/C
(A7) C7
(Em9/A) Gm9/C
(Em7/A) Gm7/C
div.
(A7) C7
(D) F
(G/D) B♭/F
D.C.
D.C.

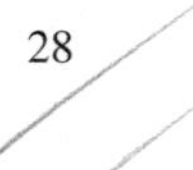

Be with me

from Psalm 91

Marty Haugen

Verses

1. You who dwell in the shel - ter of the Lord Most
2. No e - vil shall be - fall you, no pain come
3. Those who cling to the Lord live se - cure in his
Cmaj7
D
G
High, who a - bides in the sha-dow of our God.
near, for his an - gels stand close by your side.
love, lif - ted high those who trust in his name.
div.
G7
C
D
G
E7

Say to the Lord: 'My refuge and fortress, the
Guarding you always and bearing you gently,
Call on the Lord, he will never forsake you, He will
Am7
D
G
C
D.C.
God in whom I trust.
D.C.
watch - in o - ver your life.
D.C.
bring you sal - va - tion and joy.
D.C.
Am7
B7
Em
E7
D.C.

The Light of Christ

Based on the Exsultet

Marty Haugen

Opening Dialogue

♩= 76
Refrain
Choir
us The Light of Christ sur-rounds us, the
mp
steady, with increasing intensity
simile
Love of Christ en-folds us, the Power of Christ pro - tects us, the
f
Last time to Coda
Vv.1-3 below; v.4 on next page
Pre - sence of Christ wat - ches o - ver us.
rit.
Last time to Coda
mp
Verses 1-3
1. All the earth is a - blaze with the glo - ry of God, for the
2. Let us fill ev - ry space with the sound of our joy, prai-sing
3. As this can - dle shines out through the dark - ness of night, may the
a tempo

Choir/Assembly
Light has come to burn a-way the dark-ness. The
Christ, who is li-ving now a-mong us.
love of Christ burn ev-er in our hearts.
Verse 4 solo
4. In the East, the Mor-ning Star ri-ses bright u-pon you, in its
peace-ful light shines the glo-ry of the Lord.
D.S. al Coda
Coda
us, for
e-ver, and e-ver, and e-ver, and e-ver. A-men!
fff

Your love is finer than life

Psalm 63: 1-2.4-5.7-8

Marty Haugen

1. As a dry and wea - ry des - ert land, so my soul is thirst - ing for my
2. I think of you when at night I rest, I re - flect up - on your stead-fast
3. I will bless your name all the days I live, I will raise my hands and call on
(Em7) F♯m7
(A7/E) B7/F♯
(Am7/E) Bm7/F♯
(Bm7) C♯m7
God, and my flesh is faint for the God I seek, for your
love, I will cling to you, O Lord my God, in the
you, my joy - ful lips shall sing your praise, you a -
(E) F♯
(Em7) F♯m7
(A7/E) B7/F♯
D.C.
love is more to me than life.
shad - ow of your wings I sing.
lone have filled my hun - gry soul.
(Am7/C) Bm7/D
(F#m7(♭5)) G♯m7(♭5)
(Am6/B) Bm6/C♯
(B7) C♯7
D.C.

Sing out, earth and skies

Words and music by Marty Haugen

Refrain

D G D G D A D
Sing out, earth and skies! Sing of the God who made us.
Sing out, earth and skies! Sing of the God who
D G D C Am7
Raise your joy - ful cries! Dance to the life a -
made you1 Raise your dance to the life a -
D C Am7 D
round you.
round you.

Bring forth the kingdom

Vv1-2: Matthew 5:13-14

Marty Haugen

 Octavo no: G-3592 (SGAU)

Refrain

Bring forth the King-dom of mer-cy, Bring forth the King-dom of peace; Bring forth the
Harmony:
G D/F♯ A D G D/F♯ A D G D/F♯
1-3: D.S.
King-dom of jus-tice, Bring forth the Ci-ty of God!
1-3: D.S.
A D G D/F♯ A D G D A D

Song of St Patrick

Based on St Patrick's Breastplate

Marty Haugen

G Dm F C Dm B♭ C Dm
be e-ver be-fore us. you Christ be e-ver be-hind us, you Christ, be e-ver with-in,
B♭ C Dm
To Refrain
Verses 2-5
Dm C Dm F G A
2. Christ u-pon our your left hand watch-ing, at our your right hand gui-ding,
3. Christ be in each ho-ly si-lence, Christ be in our your spea-king,
4. Let May us you be God's light in the dark-ness, let may us you be God's kind-ness,
5. God Cre-a-tor, bless and keep us, you, Christ, be ev-er near us; you;
Dm F C Dm B♭ C Dm
Christ ab-ove, be-neath us you guar-ding, near to us a-bi-ding.
Christ in ev-ery work we you of-fer, ev-er in our your see-king.
Let may us you be God's jus-tice and mer-cy, hands and feet of Christ.
Spi-rit, be the light be-fore us; you; gen-tle be our your path-way.
B♭ C Dm
To Refrain

Healer of our every ill

Words and music by Marty Haugen

peace and glad - ness, Spir - it of all com - fort: fill our
still un - fold - ing, give us all your vi - sion: God of
ev - 'ry broth - er, Spir - it of all kind - ness: be our
way of heal - ing, Spir - it of com - pas - sion: fill each
(E♭) F (Dm) Em (C/E) D/F♯ (F) G (Am) Bm
D.C. Coda
hearts. sor - row.
love.
guide.
heart.
(G/B) A/C♯ (F/A) G/B (G) A D.C. (G/B) A/C♯ (Am) Bm (F) G (Dm) Em G/B A/C♯
(C) D (C7) D7 (F/C) G/D (Fm6/C) Gm6/D (C) D (C7) D7 (F/C) G/D (Fm6/C) Gm6/D (C) D Fine

Shepherd me, O God

Psalm 23

Marty Haugen

Verses 1, 2, 3
1. God is my shep - herd, so noth - ing shall I want, I rest in the mead - ows of faith - ful - ness and love, I walk by the qui - et wa - ters of peace.
2. Gent - ly you raise me and heal my wea - ry soul, you lead me by path - ways of right - eous - ness and truth, my spir - it shall sing the mu - sic of your name.
3. Though I should wan - der the val - ley of death, I fear no e - vil, for you are at my side, your rod and your staff, my com - fort and my hope.
(Em) Fm
(Am/E) B♭m/F
(Em7) Fm7
(A/E) B♭/F
(Am7) B♭m7
(Bm7) Cm7
(Am/C) B♭m/D♭
(D) E♭
D.S.

Verse 4
f
4. You have set me a ban - quet of love
(Am)
B♭m
(D)
E♭
in the face of ha - tred,
crown-ing me with
pp unis.
(G)
A♭
(C)
D♭
(Am)
B♭m
(Am7/G)
B♭m7/A♭
pp
love be - yond my pow'r to hold.
rit.
D.S.
(F#m7-5)
Gm7-5
(B7)
C7
rit.
Verse 5
p
5. Sure - ly your kind - ness and mer - cy fol - low me all the days of my
(Em)
Fm
(Am/E)
B♭m/F
(Em7)
Fm7
(A/E)
B♭/F
(Am7)
B♭m7
(Bm7)
Cm7
p

poco rit.
a tempo
life; I will dwell in the house of my God for ev - er - more.
(Asus4) Bbsus 4
(A) Bb
(Am7) Bbm7
(Bm7) Cm7
(C) Db
(D) Eb
(Em) Fm
(Am/E) Bbm/F
poco rit.
a tempo
Final Refrain
p a bit slower
Shep - herd me, O God, be- yond my wants, be-
(Em7) Fm7
(A/E Bb/F
(Em) Fm
(C) Db
(G) Ab
(D) Eb
p a bit slower
yond my fears, from death in - to life.
(Bm7) Cm7
(C) Db
(Am7) Bbm7
(Bm7) Cm7
(C) Db
(D) Eb
(Em) Fm
(Am/E) Bbm/F
(E) F

Now in this banquet

Words and music by Marty Haugen

 Octavo no: G-2918 (SGAU)

To verses
(Am7/G) (D) (G) (Am7/G) (D) (G) (Am7/G) (D/F♯)
B♭m7/A♭ E♭ A♭7 B♭m7/A♭ E♭ A♭ B♭m7/A♭ E♭/G
poured, Love is the sign of our Lord.
day, Wis - dom to walk in your way.
grace, One in your lov - ing em– brace.
Last time
(G) (Am7/G) (D/G) (G) (C/G) (G)
A♭ B♭m7/A♭ E♭/A♭ A♭ D♭/A♭ A♭
Lord.
way.
brace.
Verses 1-2
(Em) (Bm) (F) (G)
Fm Cm G♭ A♭
1. You who have touched us and graced us with love,
2. Let our hearts burn with the fire of your love;
(C) (G/B (Am7) (F) (D/F♯
D♭ A♭/C B♭m7 G♭ E♭/G
D.S.
make us your peo - ple of good - ness and light.
o - pen our eyes to the glo - ry of God.

Verse 3
(Em)
Fm
(C)
D♭
(F)
G♭
(Em7)
Fm7
3. God who makes the blind to see, God who makes the lame to walk,
(Am7)
B♭m7
(G/B)
A♭/C
(C)
D♭
(D)
E♭
D.S.
bring us danc-ing in-to day, lead your peo-ple in your way.
Verse 4
(Em7)
Fm7
(C)
D♭
(F)
G♭
(Em7)
Fm7
4. Hope for the hope-less, light for the blind,
(Am7)
B♭m7
(G/B
A♭/C
(C)
D♭
(F)
G♭
rit.
(D/F♯)
E♭/G
D.S.
'Strong' is your name, Lord, 'Gen-tle' and 'Kind.'
rit.

Verse 5
(Em7) Fm7
(Am7) B♭m7
(D/F♯) E♭/G
(G) A♭
5. Call us to be your light, call us to be your love,
(E♭) E
(A♭/C) A/C♯
(Am7) B♭m7
(D) E♭
D.S.
make us your peo - ple a - gain.
(Em7) Fm7
(G7) A♭7
(C) D♭
(G/B) A♭/C
6. Come, O Spir - it! re - new our hearts!
(Am7) B♭m7
(G/B) A♭/C
(C) D♭
(F) G♭
rit.
(D/F♯) E♭/G
D.S.
We shall a - rise to be chil-dren of light.
rit.

Easter Alleluia

Words by Marty Haugen

O FILII ET FILIAE, French, 15th century.
adapted by Marty Haugen

prais - es now sing, All of cre - a - tion in splen-dour shall ring:
life has be - gun, Life now per - fect - ed in Je - sus, the Son:
all of us here, Fill us with joy and cast out all our fear:
all that we do, We would the gate of sal - va - tion pass through:
fol - low your way, You are the pot - ter and we are the clay:
fire___ and sword, Fill us with love and the peace of his word:
(D) F (Em) Gm (C) E♭ (Am) Cm (Em) Gm (Bm7) Dm7
D.C.
Al - le - lu - ia!
(D) F (G) B♭ (D) F (Em) Gm (Esus4) Gsus4 (Em) Gm (Esus4) Gsus4
D.C.
Coda
al - le - lu - ia!
(D) F (G) B♭ (D) F (Em) Gm (Esus4) E♭msus4 (Em) Gm (Esus4) E♭msus4 (Em) Gm (Esus4) Gsus4 (Em) Gm

God of Day and God of Darkness

Words by Marty Haugen

BEACH SPRING, 8787D. *The Sacred Harp,* 1844
arranged by Marty Haugen

 Octavo no: G-3595 (SGAU)

Awake, O Sleeper

Ephesians 5:8.14

Marty Haugen

Final ending
D/A
Am7/G
ff
Dm7
Em7
A(add 9)
light; and Christ will fill you with light.
Verses 1, 2
Fmaj7
G Am G Am
1. Once you were dark-ness, once you were lost in the shadows,
2. Live as God's peo-ple, live as God's jus-tice and mer-cy,
G Am G Am G Fmaj7 G
Once you were dark-ness, now you are
Filled with com-pas-sion, filled with the
D/A Am7/G D.S.
chil-dren of light.
po-wer of love.

 Octavo no: G-2918 (SMG)

Blest are those who love you

Psalm 128

Marty Haugen

UK agent Decani Music, Oak House, 70 High Street, Brandon IP27 0AU. **Octavo no:** G-3336 (PsChY2)

Refrain II
May the Lord bless us,
May the Lord pro - tect us,
(D) F
(Em7/D) Gm7/F
(Bm7) Dm7
(E7) G7
To verses
all the days,
all the days of our life.
(Em9) Gm9
(Em7/A) Gm7/C
(D) F
(Edim7/D) Gdim7/F
Final ending
(Edim7/D) Gdim7/F
(D7) F7
(Em7/D) Gm7/F
(Edim7/D) Gdim7/F
(D) F

Verses

1. Hap - py all those who fear the Lord, and walk in God's path - way;
2. Your spouse shall be like a fruit-ful vine in the midst of your home, your
3. May the bless - ings of God be yours all the days of your life,
(D) F
(G/D) B♭/F
(Bm7) Dm7
(E) G
To refrain
you will find what you long for: the rich-es of our God.
chil-dren flour - ish like ol - ive plants re - joic-ing at your ta - ble.
may the peace and the love of God live al-ways in your heart.
(G) B♭
(D/F♯) F/A
(Gm) B♭m
(A) C

Like a deer

Psalms 42, 43

Marty Haugen

Response
Like a deer that longs for running streams, my soul is longing for you; thirsting for you. my God.
Bm7 Em Em7/D A/C♯ Am7
D A Am7 Bm7 D Am/E E
To verses
Last time to CODA
Coda
thirs - ting for you. my God.
Am7 Bm7 D Am/E E

Verses
1. My soul thirsts for God, for the li - ving God;
2. I go with the throng to the house of God;
3. Send forth your light and your truth, O God;
4. Then will I go to the al - tar of God;
When shall I come and be - hold (the) the face of God?
with cries of our joy, and our songs (of) of thanks and praise.
Bring me at last to your ho (-ly) ly dwel - ling place.
come in - to the God of my glad - (ness) ness and my joy.
D G C G/B
A Em D/F♯ G A7
Em/B B7 Em Em7/D A/C♯ Am/C
D.S.

Send down the fire

Marty Haugen

To verses
life in your peo - ple and make us the peo - ple of God.
(D) E♭ (F#7) G7 (Bm) Cm (Em) Fm (D/F♯) E♭/G (G) A♭ (A) B♭ (D) E♭ (A) B♭ (G) A♭ (A) B♭
Final (or jump to **)
God, and we shall be peo - ple of God.
(Bm7) Cm7 (E7) F7 (Em7) Fm7 (D/F♯) E♭/G (G) A♭ (A) B♭ (D) E♭ (A) B♭
no rit.
(G) A♭ (A) B♭ (D) E♭ (A) B♭ (G) A♭ (A) B♭ (G) A♭ (A) B♭ (D) E♭

 Octavo no: G-3915 (TOW)

Carol at the Manger

Marty Haugen

 Octavo no: G-3572 (NOS/WC). Introduction and *Joyous Light* (opposite) from HEP (G-3460)

(Bm) Cm (A) B♭ (G) A♭ (D) E♭ (Em7) Fm7 (A7) B♭7 (D) E♭
Last time to Coda
taught us love un - spo - ken, teach us now where you are found.
fire of your com-pas - sion kin - dle ev - 'ry land and race.
hearts might be for - giv - ing and our spir - its strong and true.

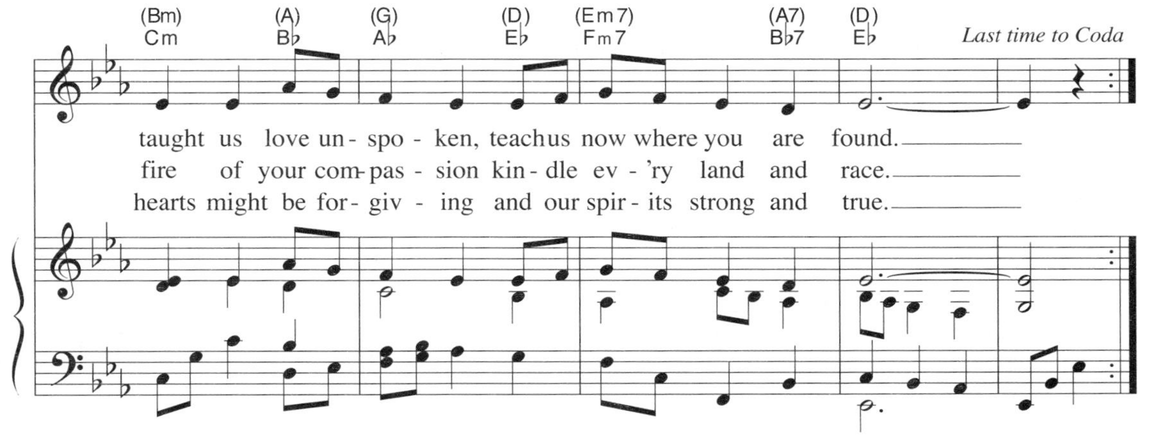

Introduction and Hymn: Holden Evening Prayer

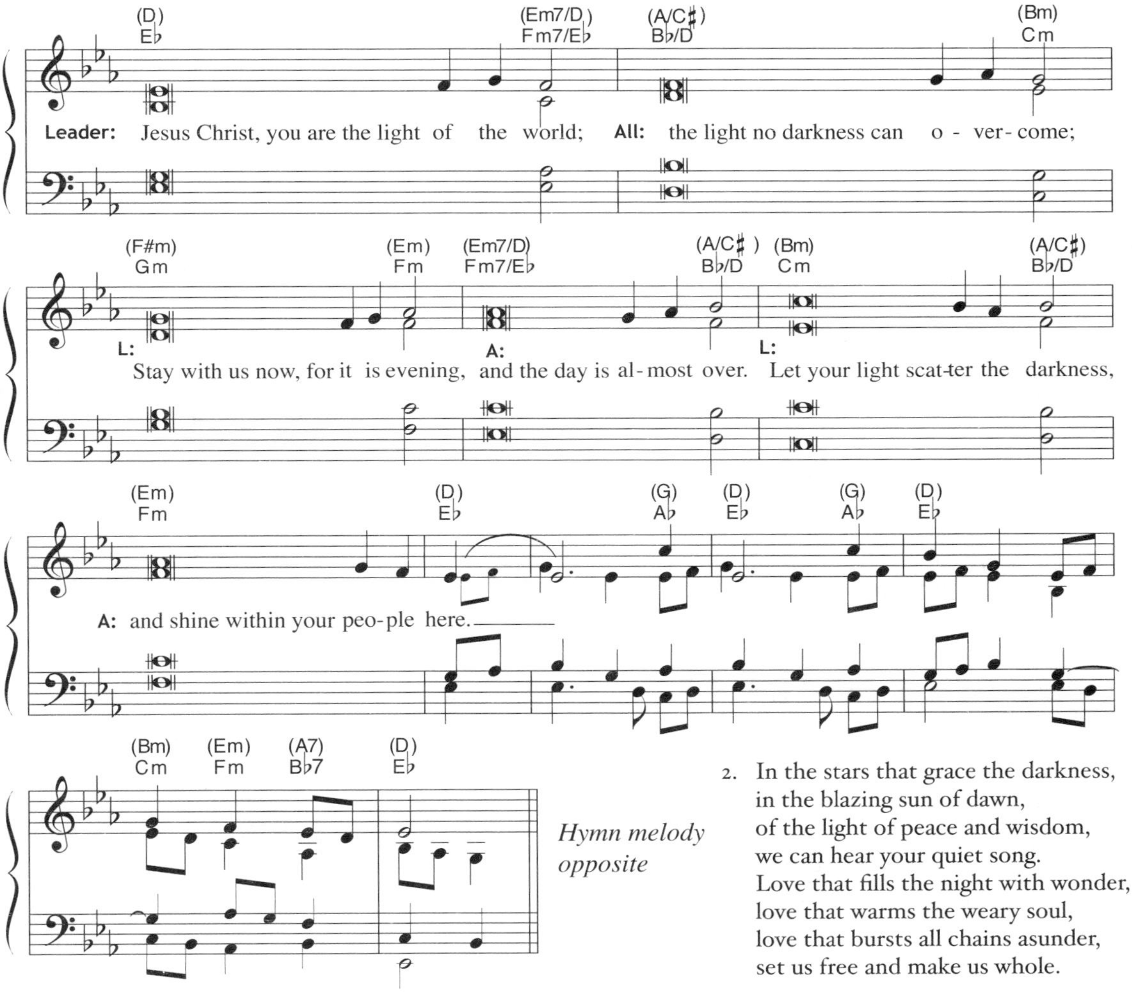

(D) E♭ (Em7/D) Fm7/E♭ (A/C♯) B♭/D (Bm) Cm
Leader: Jesus Christ, you are the light of the world; All: the light no darkness can o - ver - come;
(F#m) Gm (Em) Fm (Em7/D) Fm7/E♭ (A/C♯) B♭/D (Bm) Cm (A/C♯) B♭/D
L: Stay with us now, for it is evening, A: and the day is al - most over. L: Let your light scat-ter the darkness,
(Em) Fm (D) E♭ (G) A♭ (D) E♭ (G) A♭ (D) E♭
A: and shine within your peo - ple here.
(Bm) Cm (Em) Fm (A7) B♭7 (D) E♭

Hymn melody opposite

1. Joyous light of heav'nly glory,
loving glow of God's own face,
you who sing creation's story,
shine on ev'ry land and race.
Now as evening falls around us,
we shall raise our songs to you,
God of daybreak, God of shadows,
come and light our hearts anew.

2. In the stars that grace the darkness,
in the blazing sun of dawn,
of the light of peace and wisdom,
we can hear your quiet song.
Love that fills the night with wonder,
love that warms the weary soul,
love that bursts all chains asunder,
set us free and make us whole.

3. You who made the heaven's splendour,
ev'ry dancing star of night,
Make us shine with gentle justice,
let us each reflect your light.
Mighty God of all creation,
gentle Christ who lights our way,
Loving Spirit of salvation,
lead us on to endless day.

Psalm 141: Let my prayer rise up

From Holden Evening Prayer

Marty Haugen

UK agent Decani Music, Oak House, 70 High Street, Brandon IP27 0AU. **Octavo no:** G-3599 (also found in HEP, G-3460)

call to you, come to me now; O hear my voice when I
All or Group 2:
O God, I call to you, come to me now; O
(Dm) E♭m (C) D♭ (Am7) B♭m7 (Dm) E♭m (F) G♭ E♭ D♭ (Dm) E♭m
cry to you.
Refrain
Let my prayer rise up like
hear my voice when I cry to you. Let my prayer rise
(C) D♭ (Am7) B♭m7 (Dm) E♭m (C) D♭ (Am7) B♭m7 (Dm) E♭m (Am7) B♭m7 (Dm) E♭m
in - cense be - fore you, the lift ing up of my hands as an
up like in - cense be - fore you, the lift ing up of my
(F) G♭ E♭ D♭ (Dm) E♭m (F) G♭ (C) D♭ (Gm) A♭m

Verse 2:
of-fer-ing to you. Keep watch with - in me, God:
hands as an of-fer-ing to you. Keep
(Gm) A♭m (Am7) B♭m7 (Dm) E♭m (C) D♭ (Am7) B♭m7 (Dm) E♭m
deep in my heart may the light of your love be burn - ing
watch with - in me, God: deep in my heart may the light of your
(C) D♭ (Am7) B♭m7 (Dm) E♭m E♭ D♭ (Dm) E♭m (C) D♭
Refrain
bright. Let my prayer rise up like in - cense be -
love be burn - ing bright. Let my prayer rise up like
(Dm) E♭m (Dm) E♭m (Am7) B♭m7 (Dm) E♭m (F) G♭ E♭ D♭

fore you, the lift-ing up of my hands as an of-fer-ing to
in - cense be - fore you, the lift-ing up of my hands as an
(Dm) E♭m
(F) G♭
(C) D♭
(Gm) A♭m
(Gm) A♭m
(Am7) B♭m7
Verse 3:
you. All praise to the God of all, cre -
of-fer-ing to you. All
(Dm) E♭m
(C) D♭
(Am7) B♭m7
(Dm) E♭m
a - tor of life; all praise be to Christ and the Spi - rit of
praise to the God of all, cre - a - tor of life; all praise be to
(C) D♭
(Am7) B♭m7
(Dm) E♭m
(F) G♭
E♭ D♭
(Dm) E♭m
(C) D♭
(Am7) B♭m7

Refrain
love.
Let my prayer rise up like
Christ and the Spi - rit of love.
Let my prayer rise
(Dm) E♭m
(C) D♭
(Am7) B♭m7
(Dm) E♭m
(Am7) B♭m7
(Dm) E♭m
in - cense be - fore you, the lift-ing up of my hands as an
up like in - cense be - fore you, the lift-ing up of my
(F) G♭
E♭ D♭
(Dm) E♭m
(F) G♭
(C) D♭
(Gm) A♭m
of-fer-ing to you.
hands as an of-fer-ing to you.
(Gm) A♭m
(Am7) B♭m7
(Dm) E♭m

Litany and Prayers

From Holden Evening Prayer

Marty Haugen

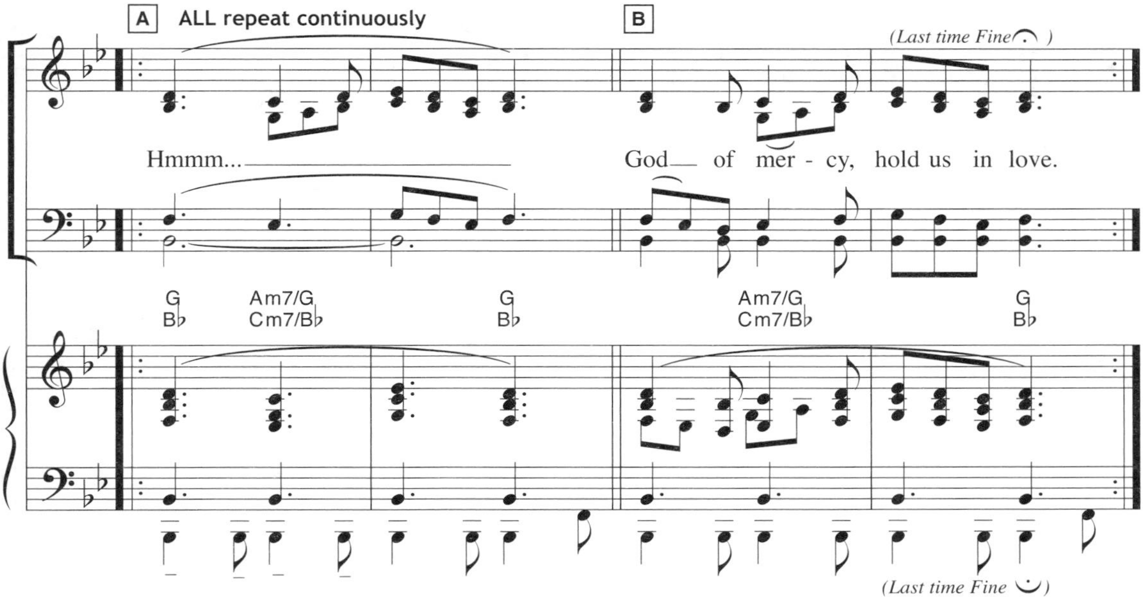

A ALL repeat continuously

B (Last time Fine)

Hmmm...

God of mer - cy, hold us in love.

G/B♭ Am7/G/Cm7/B♭ G/B♭ Am7/G/Cm7/B♭ G/B♭

(Last time Fine)

Invocations

Leader: A B

1. In peace, in peace we pray to you:
2. For peace and sal - va - tion, we pray to you.
3. For peace be - tween na - tions, for peace be - tween peo - ples:
4. For we who are ga - thered to wor - ship and praise you:
5. For all of your ser - vants who live out your gos - pel:
6. For all those who go - vern, that jus - tice might guide them:
7. For all those who la - bour in ser - vice to o - thers:
8. Grant wea - ther that nou - rish - es all of cre - a - tion:
9. Keep watch on our loved ones and keep us from dan - ger:
10. For all the be - lov - ved who rest in your mer - cy:

Conclusion accompaniment as above

A B

Leader: Help us, com - fort us, all of our days: Keep us, hold us, gra - cious God.

All you works of God

Daniel 5:57 ff

Marty Haugen

UK agent Decani Music, Oak House, 70 High Street, Brandon IP27 0AU. **Octavo no:** G-3481 (TOW)

Coda
Em7 A7 G/B C Am7 G/D D
God! Raise your voi - ces all you works of
G D C C/D D G D C C/D G
fine
God!
Verses
D G C G D G
Solo: Sun and moon: All: Bless your Ma - ker! S: Stars of hea-ven A: chant your praise!
Winds of God: Cold and win-ter:
Night and day: Light and darkness:
All the earth: Hills and moun-tains:
Wells and springs: Seas and ri-vers:
Fly-ing birds: Beasts and cat-tle:
All who live: Men and wo-men:
G C/F F C/E C Am7 D
D.S.
S: Sho-wers and dew: A: Raise up your joy - ful song.
Snow-storms and ice:
Light-'nings and clouds:
Green things that grow:
Whales in the deep:
Chil - dren at play:
Ser - vants of God:
D.S.

Return to God

Amos 5:21-24

Marty Haugen

Coda
Descant:
Come, seek the ten - der faith-ful-ness of God.
faith-ful-ness of God.
D G/B Am7/C Bm7 G/B Am6/E E
Verses 1, 2
1. Now the time of grace has come, the day of sal - va - tion; come and learn now the way of our God.
2. I will take your heart of stone and place a heart with - in you, a heart of com-pas-sion and love.
Am D Gmaj7
C Am Am7/C B Am/B B7
D.S.

Verse 3
3. If you break the chains of op - pres - sion, if you set the pris - 'ner
if you share your bread with the hun - gry, give pro - tec - tion to the
give a shel - ter to the home - less, clothe the na - ked in your
F♯m6/E
Em
F♯m7/E
1.2
3
free;
lost;
midst,
then your light shall break forth like the
Em
Em
Cmaj7
Am7
dawn.
D.S.
E
Am7/G
F♯m7/E
B7
D.S.

Let justice roll like a river

Amos 5:21-24, 8:4;
Micah 4:3-4.6.8; Joel 2:12-14

Marty Haugen

take us, move and shake us, Come now, and make us a - new,
(G/B) B♭/D
(Am7) Cm7
(G/B) B♭/D
(C) E♭
(A7/E) C7/E
(C) E♭/F
that we might live just - ly like you.
To verses
Last time
(D) F
(Am7) Cm7
(D7) F7
(G) B♭
(C) E♭
(G) B♭
(B7) D7/A
(G) B♭
Verse 1
(Em) Gm
(B7) D7/A
(Em) Gm/B♭
(B7) D7/A
(Em) Gm
(C) E♭
(D) F
1. Take from me your ho - ly feasts, all your of - f'rings and your

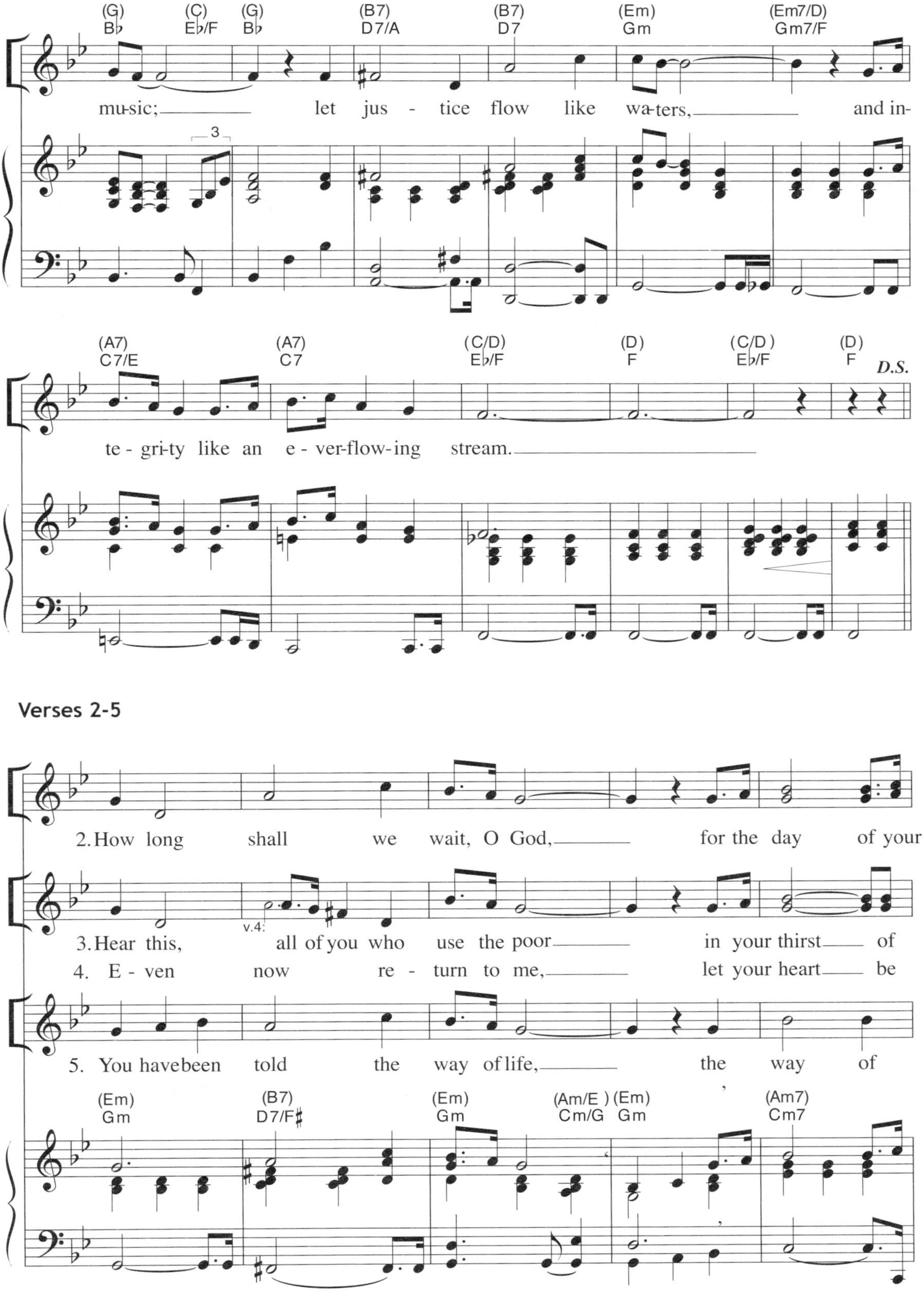

(G) B♭ (C) E♭/F (G) B♭ (B7) D7/A (B7) D7 (Em) Gm (Em7/D) Gm7/F

music; let jus - tice flow like wa-ters, and in-

3

(A7) C7/E (A7) C7 (C/D) E♭/F (D) F (C/D) E♭/F (D) F *D.S.*

te - gri-ty like an e - ver-flow-ing stream.

Verses 2-5

mer - cy to dawn, the day we beat our
po - wer and ri - ches; the Lord will turn your
bro - ken and hum - ble, for I am gra - cious,
jus - tice and peace; to act just - ly, to
(D) F
(G) B♭
(B7) D7/A
(Em) Gm
(B7) D7/F♯
Vv. 3-4
D.S.
swords in - to ploughs, when your peace reigns o - ver the earth!
laughter to tears, on the won - drous Day of our God.
gen-erous and kind; come and seek the mer-cies of God.
love gen - tly, and walk hum-bly with God
(G/D) B♭/F
(Adim/C) Cdim/E♭
(G/D) B♭/F
(A7) C7/G
(A7) C7
(C/D) E♭/F
(D) F
D.S.

Come to the feast

Refrain: Isaiah 55:1

Marty Haugen

 Octavo no: G-3453 (WL)

1
2
All:
For
end to hun - ger:
have no mon - ey:
share the rich - es:
end to sad - ness:
One who calls you: Come to the feast! Come to the feast!
Cup that saves you:
feast of free - dom:
feast with cour - age:
feast of jus - tice:
feast of heal - ing: Come to the feast! Come to the feast! For
Am7 G/B Am7 D7 G Am7 D7 G
this is life:
Solo or S, A:
All:
For this is
this is life: 1. the wa - ters of the Jor - dan: this is
2. the streams of joy and glad - ness:
3. the floods that o - ver- whelm you:
4. the wa - ters that have freed you:
this is life: 5. to die and rise in Je - sus: For this is
Am7 D G D/F♯ Em Am7

life:
Solo or S, A:
All:
For this is
life: the wa - ters of your birth: this is
the rains that bring you joy:
the streams of death and life:
the sav - ing stream of God:
life: to share the life of Christ: For this is
D G G7 Am7
life:
Solo or S, A:
life: the wa - ters that re - new you:
the wa - ters that re - store you:
the wa - ters that sus - tain you: O come to the
to share a - round the ta - ble:
life: the bread and wine of jus - tice:
D B7 Em C D
All:
1-4
5
feast. O come to the feast, feast, O come to the feast.
Em G/D Am7 D G Em Am7 D7 G

How long, O God

Verses from Pss. 13 and 22

Marty Haugen

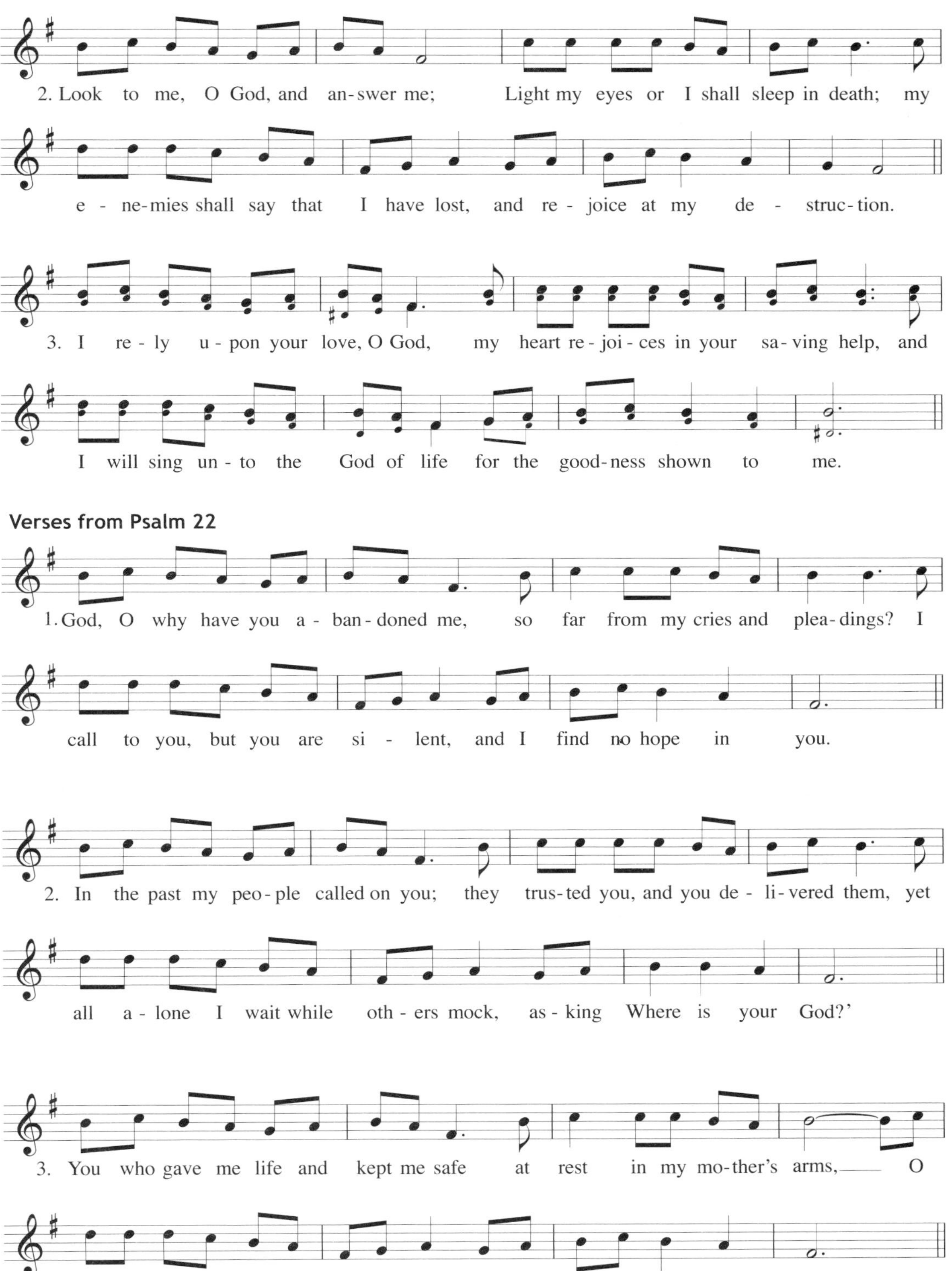
2. Look to me, O God, and an-swer me; Light my eyes or I shall sleep in death; my
e - ne-mies shall say that I have lost, and re - joice at my de - struc-tion.
3. I re - ly u - pon your love, O God, my heart re - joi - ces in your sa-ving help, and
I will sing un - to the God of life for the good-ness shown to me.
Verses from Psalm 22
1. God, O why have you a - ban-doned me, so far from my cries and plea-dings? I
call to you, but you are si - lent, and I find no hope in you.
2. In the past my peo-ple called on you; they trus-ted you, and you de - li-vered them, yet
all a - lone I wait while oth - ers mock, as - king Where is your God?'
3. You who gave me life and kept me safe at rest in my mo-ther's arms, O
be not far from me for I am faint, there is no - one near to help.

Who will speak?

Refrain adopted from a homily
by Mgr Ray East

Marty Haugen

Refrain: Who will *speak__ if we/you__ don't?
Verse: Ooh__

Verses

1. Who will speak__ for the poor and the bro - ken?
2. Who will speak__ for the ones who are voice - less?
3. Who will speak__ for the chil - dren of vio - lence?
4. Who will speak__ for the shunned and the out - cast?
5. Who will work__ for the thou - sands of home - less?
6. Who will care__ for the plants and the crea - tures?
7. Who will care__ for the weak and the a - ged?

Capo 3: (C) E♭ (F) A♭ (C/G) E♭/B♭ (G7) B♭7

* *use speak, work or care according to preceding verse*

Who will *speak__ if we/you__ don't? Who will *speak__ so their
Ooh__ Ooh__

Who will speak__ for the peo- ples op- pressed? Who will *speak__ so their
Speak the truth__ in the pla- ces of power?
Who will speak__ for the wo- men a - bused?
Who will speak__ for all peo- ple with AIDS?
Who will work__ in the ghet- tos and streets?
Who will care__ for the land and the sea?
Who will care__ for the ones with no hope?

(Dm) Fm (Dm/G) Fm/B♭ (C) E♭ (C7) E♭7

To key change after v. 4, 5 or 6
voice will be heard? Oh who will *speak if we/you don't?
(ooh)
voice will be heard? Oh who will *speak if we/you don't?
(F) A♭
(Fm/A♭) A♭m/C♭
(C/G) E♭/B♭
To key change after v. 4, 5 or 6
(C) E♭
a capella first time - optional
don't?
Refrain: Who will *speak if we/you don't?
Verse: Ooh
(C) E♭
(A/C♯) C/E
(D) F
(G) B♭
(D/A) F/C
(A7) C7
Who will *speak if we/you don't?
Ooh
Who will *speak so their
Ooh
(Em) Gm
(Em/A) Gm/C
(D) F
8va
(D7) F7

 Octavo no: G-3963 (AG/IDC)

Psalm 63: In the morning I will sing

Words from the Grail version

Marty Haugen

 Octavo no: G-4276 (AW)

Verses
1. O God, you are my God, for you I long; for you my soul is thir-sting. My bo-dy pines for you like a
2. For your love is bet-ter than life, my lips will speak your praise. So I will bless you all my life, in your
3. On my bed I re-mem-ber you, on you I muse through the night; for you have been my help; in the
D
Gadd9
Bm
Em
A7
D
Alternative Refrain
My soul is thir-sting for you, my soul is thirs-ting for
A7
D
Gm6/D
D
F♯m7
G

dry, wea-ry land with-out wa-ter. So I gaze on you in the
name I will lift up my hands. My soul shall be filled as with a
sha-dow of your wings I re - joice. My soul clings to
Fmaj7 Gm7 D D7/C
sanc tu-a-ry to see your strength and your glo-ry.
D.C.
ban - quet, my mouth shall praise you with joy.
you; your right hand holds me fast.
G/B Gm/B♭ C Am7 D
Last time rit.
To verses
Final
you, O Lord my God, thirs-ting for you, my God. God.
A F♯7/A♯ Bm D D/A Gmaj7/A A D D

Springs of water

Words and music by Marty Haugen

formed you! Sound from your depths a hymn that tells the won - ders God has done!
bogs! Rich with the life that God cre - ates, now let your song be heard!
life! Danc - ing with joy from peak to val - ley, laugh-ing and clear your song!
wa - ters! Show - er the earth with life and good - ness, show - er the grace of God!
O bless - ed be God for ev - er!
All: Bless-ed be God for ev - er!
D.C.
(Fmaj 7) A♭maj 7
(Dm7) Fm7
(G7) B♭7
(F) A♭
(C/E) E♭/G
(G7) B♭7
(Am) Cm
(Dm7) Fm7
(C/E) E♭/G
(G7) B♭7
(C) E♭

All are welcome

Words and music by Marty Haugen

A place where saints and chil - dren tell how hearts learn to for - give.
Where all God's chil - dren dare to seek to dream God's reign a - new.
A ban - quet hall on ho - ly ground, where peace and jus - tice meet.
to heal and strength - en, serve and teach, and live the Word they've known.
and loved and treas - ured, taught and claimed as words with - in the Word.
Built of hopes and dreams and vi - sions, Rock of faith and vault of
Here the cross shall stand as wit - ness and as sym - bol of God's
Here the love of God, through Je - sus, is re - vealed in time and
Here the out - cast and the stran - ger bear the im - age of God's
Built of tears and cries and laugh - ter, prayers of faith and songs of
(D/F♯) F/A (Bm7) Dm7 (Em) Gm (A) C (Em7) Gm7 (D/F♯) F/A (G) B♭ (A7) C7
(G/D) B♭/F (A) C (F#m7) Am7 (Bm7) Dm7 (Em7) Gm7 (A) C (D) F (D/F♯) F/A

grace; Here the love of Christ shall end di - vi - sions:
grace; Here as one we claim the faith of Je - sus:
space; As we share in Christ the feast that frees us:
face; Let us bring an end to fear and dan - ger:
grace, Let this house pro-claim from floor to raf - ter:
(G) B♭ (D) F (G) B♭ (F#7) A7 (Bm) Dm
All are wel - come, all are wel - come, all are wel - come in this
(Em) Gm (Bm) Dm (F#m7) Am7 (Em/G) Gm/B♭ (D/A) F/C (Em7/A) Gm7/C (A7) C7
place.
D.S.
(D) F (G/D) B♭/F (D) F (G/D) B♭/F (D) F (G/D) B♭/F (D) F (G/A) B♭/C
Last time Fine
D.S.

Now bless the God of Israel

Luke 1:68-79, versified by Ruth Duck

Marty Haugen

On the journey to Emmaus

Words by Marty Haugen

COLUMCILLE, Irish traditional
arranged by Marty Haugen

stran - ger walks with us and, to our sur - prise, he
begged him, 'Stay with us and grant us your word.' We
van - ished be - fore us we knew he was near— the
words burn with - in us— let none be ig - nored— who
(Dm)
F♯m
(C/E)
E/G♯
(F)
A
o - pens our stor - ies and he o - pens our eyes.
wel - comed the stran - ger and we wel - comed the Lord.
life in our dy - ing and the hope in our fear.
wel - comes the stran - ger shall wel - come the Lord.
(B♭maj7)
Dmaj7
(Am7)
C♯m7
(Gm7)
Bm7
(Am7)
C♯m7
(Dm)
F♯m

Abundant Life

Words by Ruth Duck

LA GRANGE, 8787D
Marty Haugen

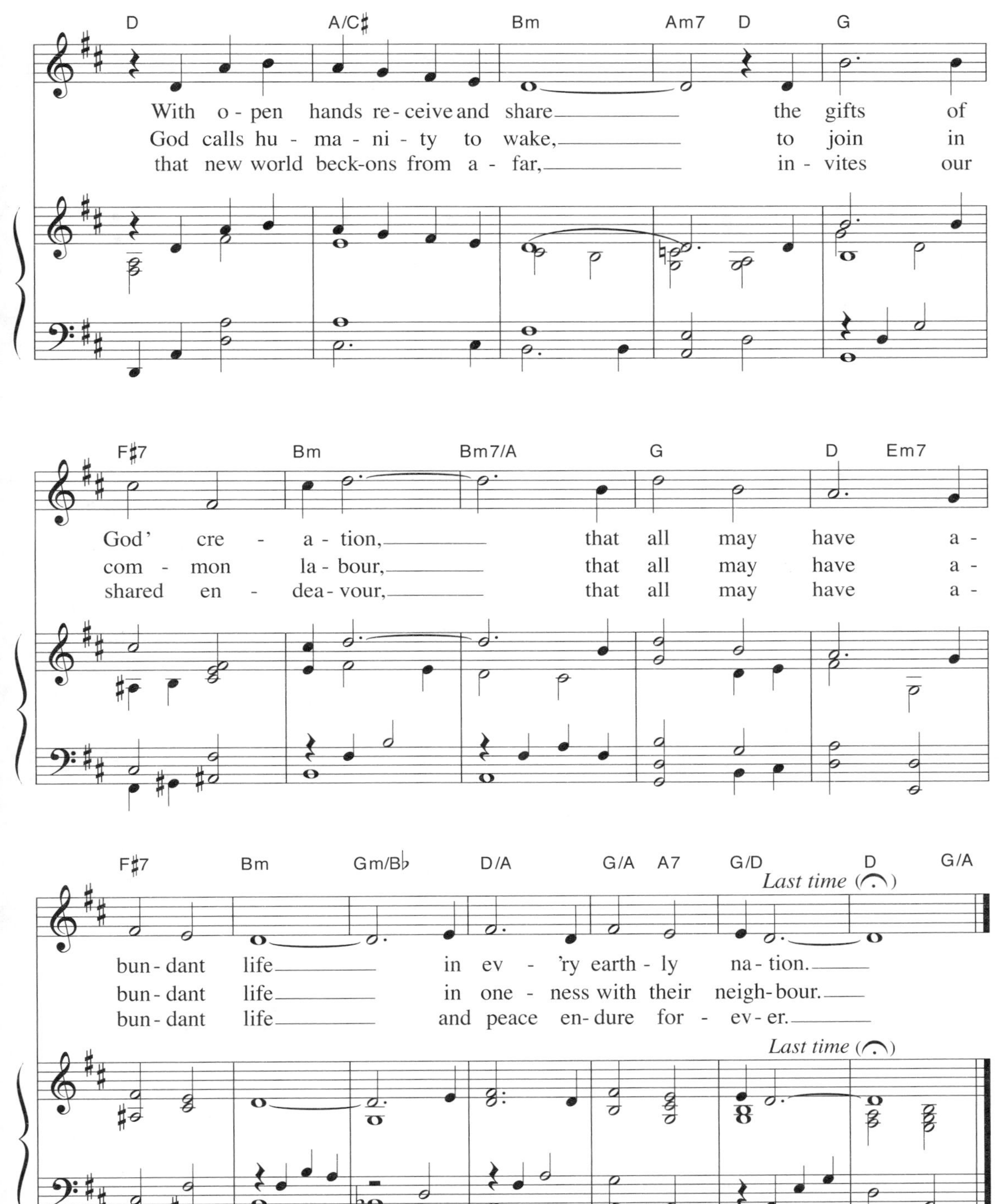
D A/C♯ Bm Am7 D G
With o - pen hands re - ceive and share the gifts of
God calls hu - ma - ni - ty to wake, to join in
that new world beck-ons from a - far, in - vites our
F♯7 Bm Bm7/A G D Em7
God' cre - a - tion, that all may have a -
com - mon la - bour, that all may have a -
shared en - dea - vour, that all may have a -
F♯7 Bm Gm/B♭ D/A G/A A7 G/D D G/A
Last time
bun - dant life in ev - 'ry earth - ly na - tion.
bun - dant life in one - ness with their neigh - bour.
bun - dant life and peace en - dure for - ev - er.
Last time

I will walk in the presence of God

Forget not what God has done

Psalm 103 Marty Haugen

 Octavo no: G-5067 (SS)

You are God (Te Deum)

4th Century Hymn

Marty Haugen

 Octavo no: G-5100 (CSJ)

Coda
a-tion wor-ships you.
Fa-ther e - ter - nal: all cre -
a-tion wor-ships you.
You are Fa - ther e - ter - nal: all cre -
Em7 G/A A Bm Bm7/A D D7 G A Bm7
a-tion wor-ships you.
a-tion wor-ships you.
Em7 G/A A D G6/D Gm6/D D
Verses 1-3
We join our hearts in praise!
Cantor
All
Cantor
1. With the an - gels in hea - ven:
With a -
2. Sing to God, our Cre - a - tor: We join our hearts in praise!
Sing to
3. Sing to Christ, King of glo - ry:
Praise his
D7 G/D Gm6/D D

Give thanks through end - less days!
All
Cantor
pos - tles and pro - phets: With the
Je - sus our Sa - viour: Give thanks through end - less days! Praise the
dy - ing and ri - sing: In his
Am/D
G/D
Gm6/D
D
One thank - ful song we raise!
D.S.
All
D.S.
church u - ni - ver - sal:
Spi - rit most Ho - ly! One thank - ful song we raise!
name is sal - va - tion:
Fmaj7
Cmaj7
Gm7
G/A
A
D.S.
Verses 4, 5
Cantor
All
4. Come then, Lord, and help your peo - ple: Come, and de - li - ver us!
5. Save your peo - ple, your in - he - ri - tance:
F♯m
Em/G
G
A

Cantor
All
Ran-somed by your ho - ly blood: Come, and de - li - ver us!
Go - vern and up - hold them al - ways!
Bm
Am7
G
A
Bring us with your saints to glo - ry: We praise your name for e - ver!
Day by day we shall bless you:
D.S.
Bm
F♯m
G
Em7
Asus4
A
D.S.

Bread to share

Based on John 6:1-15

Marty Haugen

Verses
1. Bread for ev - ry hun - ger: the
2. Bread for those who sor - row: and
3. Bread for ev - ry sis - ter: and
4. Bread of hope and kind - ness: the
5. Fish for those who hun - ger: and
6. Wine of our re - membrance: the
7. Wine of our for - give-ness: the
8. Room for those for - got - ten: and
9. Room for all the chil - dren: and
10. Room for those who suf - fer: and
Hmm you have plen - ty to share.
(D) E♭
(A7) (Bm) B♭7 Cm
bread of joy and glad - ness: the
bread of life and laugh - ter: the
bread for ev - ry bro - ther: and
bread of your com - pas - sion: the
joy for all who sor - row: and
wine of dreams and vi - sions: the
wine of our re - demp - tion: the
room for those re - jec - ted: and
room for all the el - ders: and
room for all the dy - ing: a
hmm you have plen - ty to share.
(D) E♭
(G) (A) A♭ B♭

bread of grace and mer - cy:
bread of strength and jus - tice:
bread for free - dom's jour - ney:
bread of love and wel-come:
faith for un - be - lie - vers:
wine of ce - le - bra - tion:
wine for our to - mor - row:
room for all the out - casts:
room for all the lone - ly:
room that sings of new life:
you have plen - ty to share, you have
(D7)
E♭7
(G)
A♭
(Gm/B♭)
A♭m/C♭
plen - ty of bread to share.
(D/A)
E♭/B♭
(Em7/A)
Fm7/B♭
(D)
E♭

Up from the waters

Words and music by Marty Haugen

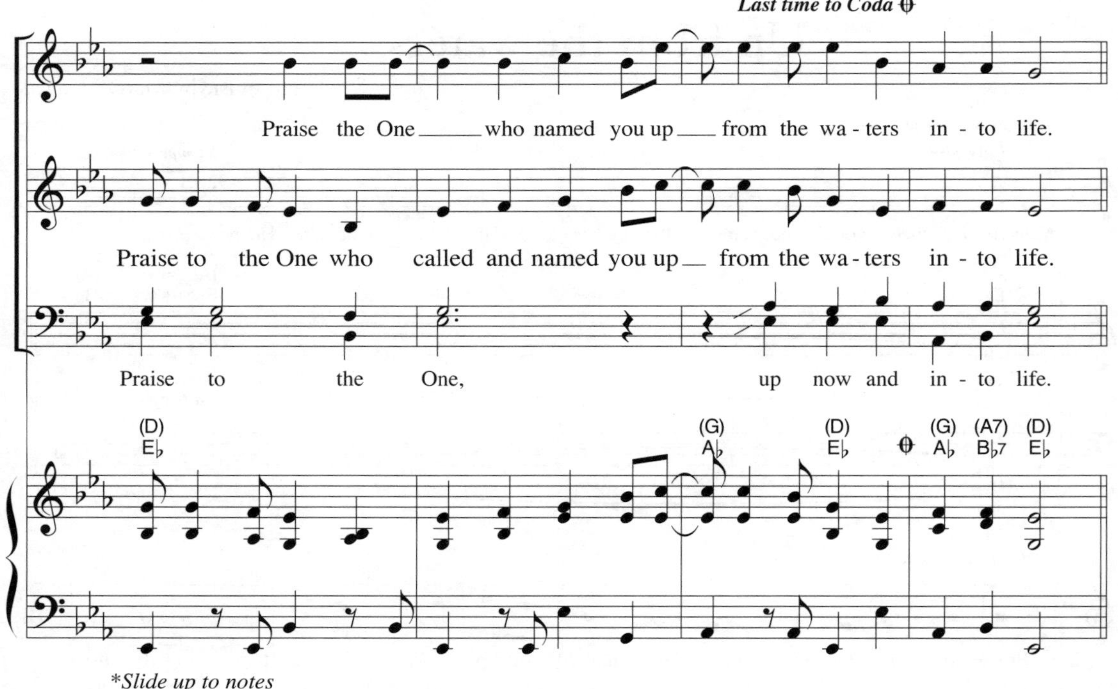

*Slide up to notes

Verses

Cantor:

All:
Up from the wa - ters in - to life.
1. How you were raised from
2. Now you be - hold God's
3. Now let the grace of
4. Now let your song ring
5. Wa - ter that heals the
6. This is the new life
Up now, O child of light. Ahom
(G) A♭ (A) B♭ (D) E♭
All:
D.S.
death in - to glo - ry: Up from the wa - ters in - to life.
mer - cy and par - don:
Je - sus en - fold you:
out with thanks - giv - ing:
heart of cre - a - tion:
Je - sus has giv - en
Up now and in - to life
(G) A♭ (A7) B♭7 (D) E♭
D.S.
Coda
1, 2
3
in - to life. Up from the wa - ters in - to life. in - to life.
in - to life. Up now and in - to life. in - to life.
(G) A♭ (A) B♭ (D) E♭ (G) A♭ (D) E♭ (G) A♭ (A) B♭ (D) E♭ (G) A♭ (A) B♭ (D) E♭
non rit.

So you must do

From John 13:1-15

Marty Haugen

 Octavo no: G-4842 (UW)

Come and eat this bread

Praise the living God

Words and music by Marty Haugen

Vv. 1-5 are to be sung during Communion. The 2nd refrain and last verse are a post-Communion thanksgiving.

To verses
Last time
breaking of the bread.
life be-yond all death.
bread.
death.
(Dm7) Fm7
(G) B♭
(Am7)(G7/B) Cm7 B♭7/D
(G) B♭
(Am7) (G7/B) Cm7 B♭7/D
(Cm) E♭m
(Dm7) Fm7
(G) B♭
Verses
1. This is the bread of life, for all to share, bread of
2. This is the cup of Christ's own sa - cri - fice, blood of
3. Just as the scat - tered grains be - come one bread, make us
4. And as we share one cup of co - ve - nant make us
5. Each time we eat this bread and drink this cup, we re -
* Now from this ta - ble to the ends of earth, ga - ther
(C) E♭
(B7) D7
(Em) Gm
(Em7/D) Gm7/F
hope and re - demp - tion, bread to feed a world of hun - gers.
love and com - pas - sion, blood to heal the world's di - vi - sions.
one in your Spi - rit, all one Bo - dy in Christ Je - sus.
one in com - mu - nion at the ta - ble of Christ Je - sus.
mem - ber your death, Lord and we ce - le - brate your ri - sing.
all of your peo - ple in this feast of all cre - a - tion.
(C) E♭
(G/B) B♭/D
(Am7) Cm7
(G/B) B♭/D
(Dsus4) Fsus4
(D) F

Within the reign of God

Marty Haugen

ho - ly food; re- ceive the bo - dy and the blood. Grace is a migh - ty flood with-
wed-ding feast, the grea - test here shall be the least. All bonds shall be re-leased
wea - ry rest, the stran - ger be a wel come guest. So shall we all be blest
seek God's face are we-lcome in this ho - ly place; join in the feast of grace
we for - get the ones who bear life's cru-shing debt; God's jus - tice guides us yet
feast is spread; in Je - sus' name we break the bread. Here shall we all be fed
ah with–
(G6/D) B♭6/F
(D) F
(A) C
(D) F
(G6/D) B♭6/F
in the reign of God.
in the reign of God. Bles-sed are they who will feast in the Reign of God,
Bles-sed, oh bles - sed
oh bles - sed
(D) F
(A) C
(D) F
(G) B♭
(D) F
(A) C
(D) F

Bles - sed are they who will share the bread of life. Bles - sed are
Bles - sed, oh
oh bles - sed oh
(G) B♭ (D) F G B♭
they who are least in the Reign of God; they shall re - joice at the feast of
bles - sed
bles - sed re - joice
(D) F (A) C (D) F (G) B♭ (D) F (Em) Gm (A7) C7
1-5
6
life.
life.
(D) F (D) F (G6/D) B♭6/F (D) F (A) C (D) F

Gathered in the love of Christ

Words adapted from Scripture

Canon in D by Johann Pachelbel (1653-1716)
adapted by Marty Haugen

 Octavo no: G-5066 (SS)

To verses
formed to be good-ness and light in the world.
formed as good-ness and light in the world.
G D G A D A Bm A
Last time
world.
world.
D A Bm D7 G D G A D
Verses
1. God is light in God there is no dark-ness. Let us walk in the
2. See what love our God has shown to us, to call us the
3. Join with me and en - ter in re - joi - cing, praise the one who has
4. Praise our God who fash-ioned all cre - a - tion: praise to Christ, who re -
1. God is light, there is no dark - ness, The
2. See what love our God has shown us, to
3. Join and en - ter in re - joi - cing, to
4. Praise our God who made cre - a - tion, to
D A Bm F♯m G D

Scripture References in the verses:

1: 1 John 1:5-8
2: 1 John 3:1, 23
3: Psalm 100

Soli Deo Gloria

Words and music by Marty Haugen

 Octavo no: G-5376 (BTL)

Gift of God

Words and music by Marty Haugen

Advent verses (general): O Antiphons

1. Come, O Wisdom, breathe within us:
   Come, O mighty tender Teacher:
   Come, and show us how to live.
2. Come, O Lord, of ancient Israel:
   You who lead us through the dsert:
   Come, and set your people free.
3. Come O Root of Jesse's lineage:
   Come, O ruler of all nations;
   Come and be our Saviour sure.

Continue overleaf

 Octavo no: G-5438 (GG)

Extra verses continued

4. Come O Holy Key of David:
Come, and open hearts to knowledge;
Come, and break the chains of death.

5. Come, O Radiant Sun of Justice:
Come, and shine on those in darkness:
All who dwell in shades of death.

6. Come, O Light of all the nations:
Come, bright Morning Star of new hope:
Come, and shine among us here.

7. Come O Living Flame of Freedom:
Living hope of our redemption:
come, and lead us to new life.

Advent Verses: Year A

Advent I 1. Bring us to God's holy mountain:
To the God of Jacob's dwelling:
Let all peoples learn your way.

2. Turn our weapons into ploughshares:
Turn our hearts from war and violence:
Let us walk in God's own light.

Advent II 3. Come, O holy Shoot of Jesse:
Come and grow within your people:
Come. O Spirit of our God.

4. You are knowledge, you are power;
you are wisdom, you are insight:
You will lead our hearts to God.

Advent III 5. Let the wilderness sing praises:
let the desert bloom in splendour;
see the glory of our God.

6. Give new strength to all the feeble:
Give new courage to the fearful:
Say, 'Be strong, for God is near.'

7. Blind will see and deaf will and hear then:
Springs will rise up in the desert:
when the day of God shall come.

Advent IV 8. God's own sign of hope and promise:
Holy Child to save all people:
Blessed one, Emmanuel.

Advent Verses: Year B

Advent I 1. Shake the nations with your presence:
Make the mountains quake and tremble:
rend the heavens and come down:

2. See us here we are your people:
We the clay and you the potter:
you have formed us, we are yours:

3. Speak the word of hope and comfort:
Cry the song of sweet forgiveness:
O Jerusalem, take heart.

Advent II 4. Make a highway in the desert:
Lift the valleys, level mountains:
let God's glory be revealed.

5. Though the people fade and wither:
Like the fragile grass and flowers:
still the Word of God endures.

6. Bring glad tidings to the lowly:
Bind up all the brokenhearted:
set the weary captives free.

Advent III 7. Come, announce a year of favour:
God's great day of vindication:
bringing joy to all who mourn.

8. God shall bring a reign of justice:
Seal a covenant of blessing:
raise a garden filled with praise.

Advent IV 9. Not in temples, dark and silent:
Not on thrones or seats of power:
with the people, God shall dwell.

10. See how God sustains and nurtures:
Grants a land of peace and safety:
for the house of Israel.

Advent Verses: Year C

Advent I 1. As our faithful God has promised;
raising up a shoot of David:
bringing justice, bringing peace.

Advent II 2. Now throw off the robes of mourning;
wear the splendour of God's glory:
wrapped in justice from our God.

3. O Jerusalem, look up now:
see your scattered children gathered:
God will lead them home in joy.

Advent III 4. Shout for joy, O daughter Zion:
let your heart be filled with gladness:
for the Lord is in your midst.

5. Do not fear or be discouraged:
now behold your mighty Saviour:
who renews your heart in love.

Advent IV 6. Out of Bethlehem a Saviour;
to be ruler over Israel:
faithful shepherd of our God.

Come, let us bring

Off. verses by Susan Briehl & Marty Haugen
Comm. verses by Billema Kwilia

Tune by Billema Kwillia
arr. by Marty Haugen

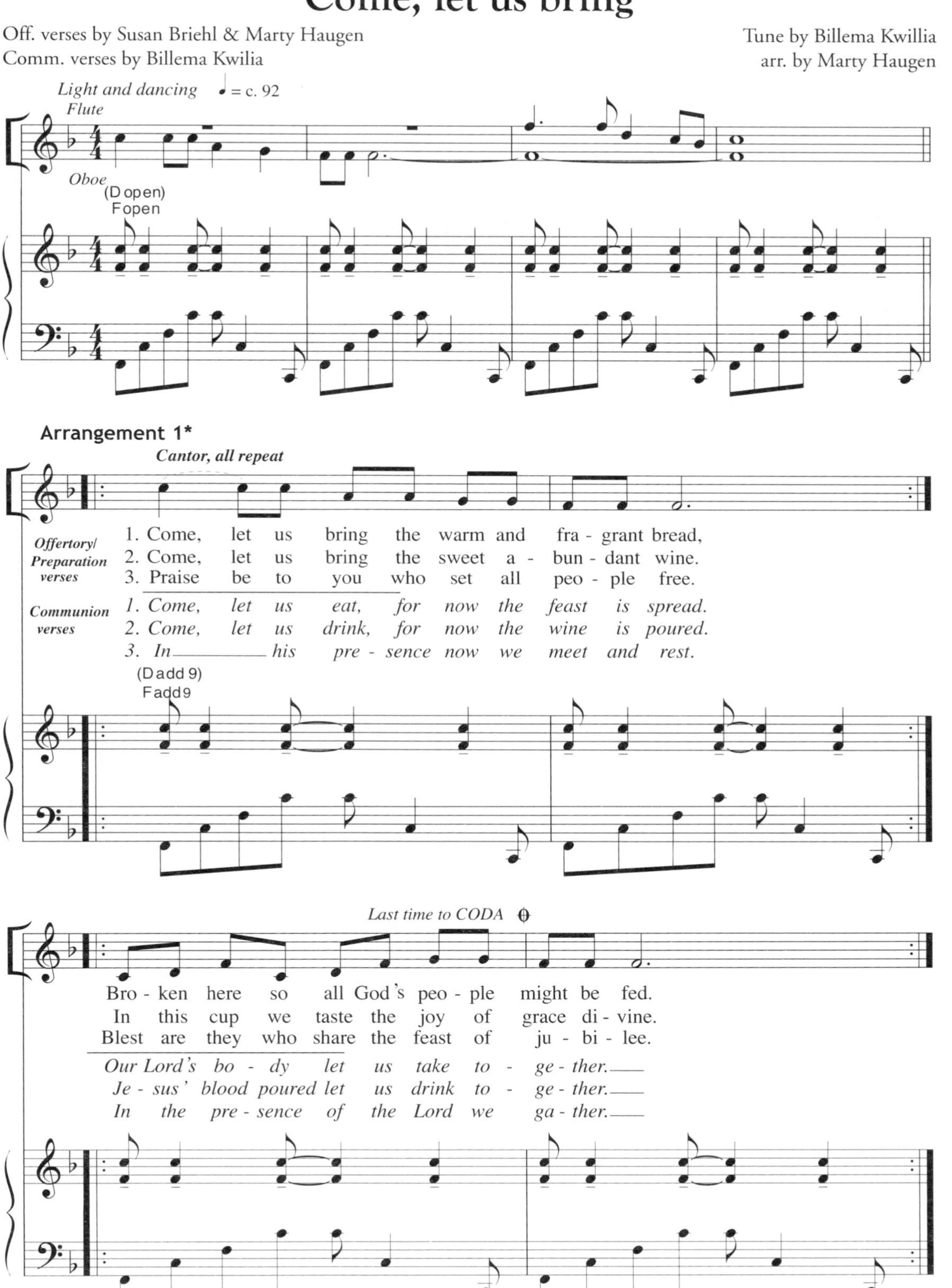

* Sing Arrangement 1 (1-3) and go to Coda. Or:
Sing Arr 1 for v.1, and proceed to Arr. 2 for vv. 2-3, and then to Coda (with optional interlude/harmony for v.3.)

Interlude
(D) F
(G6/D) B♭6/F
(D) F
(A/D) C/F
(G/A) B♭/C
Arrangement 2
Cantor/Choir
1. Come, let us bring the warm and fra - grant bread,
2. Come, let us bring the sweet a - bun - dant wine.
3. Praise be to you who set all peo - ple free.
1. Come, let us eat, for now the feast is spread.
2. Come, let us drink, for now the wine is poured.
3. In his pre - sence now we meet and rest.
All:
1. Come, let us bring the warm and
2. Come, let us bring the sweet a -
3. Praise be to you who set all
1. Come, let us eat, for now the
2. Come, let us drink, for now the
3. In his pre - sence now we

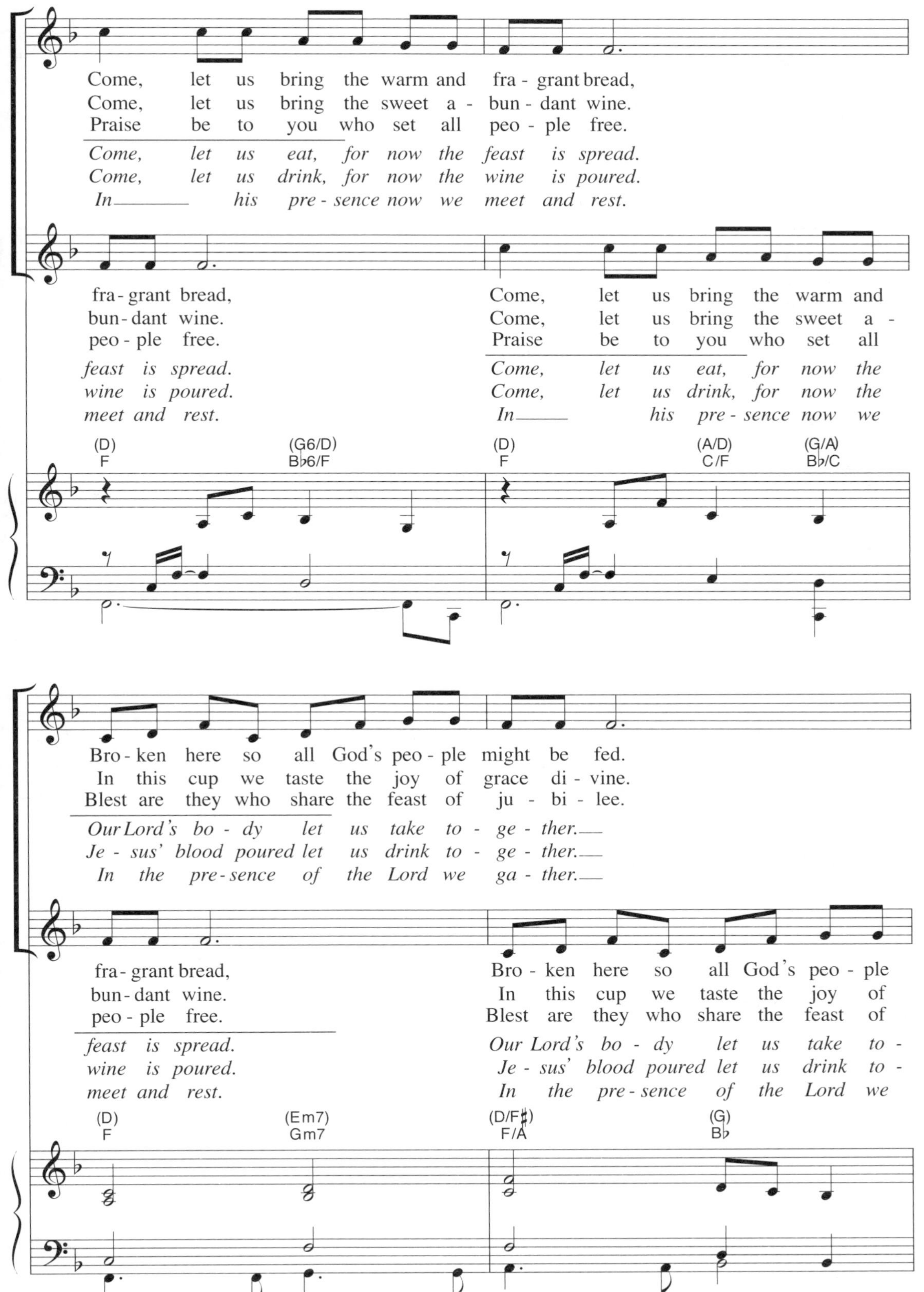
Come, let us bring the warm and fra - grant bread,
Come, let us bring the sweet a - bun - dant wine.
Praise be to you who set all peo - ple free.
Come, let us eat, for now the feast is spread.
Come, let us drink, for now the wine is poured.
In his pre - sence now we meet and rest.
fra - grant bread,
bun - dant wine.
peo - ple free.
feast is spread.
wine is poured.
meet and rest.
Come, let us bring the warm and
Come, let us bring the sweet a -
Praise be to you who set all
Come, let us eat, for now the
Come, let us drink, for now the
In his pre - sence now we
(D) F
(G6/D) B♭6/F
(D) F
(A/D) C/F
(G/A) B♭/C
Bro - ken here so all God's peo - ple might be fed.
In this cup we taste the joy of grace di - vine.
Blest are they who share the feast of ju - bi - lee.
Our Lord's bo - dy let us take to - ge - ther.
Je - sus' blood poured let us drink to - ge - ther.
In the pre - sence of the Lord we ga - ther.
fra - grant bread,
bun - dant wine.
peo - ple free.
feast is spread.
wine is poured.
meet and rest.
Bro - ken here so all God's peo - ple
In this cup we taste the joy of
Blest are they who share the feast of
Our Lord's bo - dy let us take to -
Je - sus' blood poured let us drink to -
In the pre - sence of the Lord we
(D) F
(Em7) Gm7
(D/F♯) F/A
(G) B♭

Bro-ken here so all God's peo-ple might be fed.
In this cup we taste the joy of grace di-vine.
Blest are they who share the feast of ju-bi-lee.
Our Lord's bo-dy let us take to-ge-ther.
Je-sus' blood poured let us drink to-ge-ther.
In the pre-sence of the Lord we ga-ther.
Last time to CODA
might be fed. Bro-ken here so all God's peo-ple might be fed.
grace di-vine. In this cup we taste the joy of grace di-vine. *
ju-bi-lee. Blest are they who share the feast of ju-bi-lee.
ge-ther. Our Lord's bo-dy let us take to-gether.
ge-ther. Je-sus' blood poured let us drink to-gether.
ga-ther. In the pre-sence of the Lord we gather.
(Bm7) Dm7 (G/A) B♭/C (D) F (A/D) C/F (G/A) B♭/C (D) F (G6/D) B♭6/F
* After v.2, sing v.3 in this arrangment or proceed to optional interlude/v3 below
Interlude (when proceeding to opt. v.3 harmony)
(Em7) Gm7 (D/F♯) F/A (G) B♭ (G/A) B♭/C (A7) C7
Optional Verse 3 Cantor, all repeat
1 2
3. Praise be to you who set all peo-ple free. Praise be to you who set all
3. In his pre-sence now we meet and rest. In his pre-sence now we
Optional harmony
Praise to you who set us free. Praise to you who
Pre-sence now we meet and rest. Pre-sence now we
(D) F (G6/D) B♭6/F (D) F (G6/D) B♭6/F (D) F (G6/D) B♭6/F

peo-ple free.
meet and rest.
Blest are they who share the feast of ju-bi-lee.
In the pre-sence of the Lord we ga-ther.
Blest are they who share the feast of
In the pre-sence of the Lord we
set us free.
meet and rest.
Blest to share the ju-bi-lee.
Pre - sence Lord we ga-ther.
Blest to share the
Pre - sence Lord we
(D)
F
(G6/D)
B♭6/F
(Em7)
Gm7
(D/F♯)
F/A
(G9)
B♭9
Coda
Cantor:
ju - bi - lee.
ga - ther.
Cantor, all repeat (sing once only)
Blest are they who share the feast of ju - bi - lee.
In the pre-sence of our Lord we ga - ther.
All:
Blest are they who share the feast of
In the pre-sence of our Lord we
ju - bi - lee.
ga - ther.
Blest are they who share the feast of
In the pre-sence of our Lord we
ju - bi - lee.
ga - ther.
(G/A)
B♭/C
(A7)
C7
Coda
(D open)
F open
Play 3 times
l. h.
pp

Kyrie

Marty Haugen

Ostinato II
Start singing at B
mer- cy, Christ, have mer - cy, Lord, have
A
(God).
1. On my breath and in my brea - thing, In my laugh-ter
2. In my song and in my si - lence, In my faith and
3. You who know my se - cret fai - lings, You who touch my
4. No one el - se's love can raise me, No one el - se's
5. Won-drous Love that seeks and finds me, Word that rai - ses
6. Sun of Jus - tice, shi - ning o'er me: Wind of New Life,
7. Rock of A - ges, still sup - port me: Bread of New Life,
8. Hea-ling Rain, pour down u - pon me: Li- ving Ri - ver,
(C) E♭ (Dm/C) Fm/E♭ (C) E♭ (G/B) B♭7/D (Dm) Fm (Am) Cm
mer - cy, have mer - cy on us. Lord, have
B
and my la - bour, full of joy or spent in grie- ving. I call u-pon you
in my doub-ting, in my strength and in my weak-ness:
dee-pest fee - lings, know me well, and still you love me:
touch can heal me, No one el - se's voice can free me:
and un- binds me, when our sin en- slaves and blinds me:
rush - ing round me: Life of ev - ry twig and blos- som:
still sus-tain me: Wine of Mer - cy, still re - new me:
swell a - round me: End-less Sea of Love, sur-round me:
(C7) E♭7 (F) A♭ (Fm/A♭) A♭m/C (C/G) E♭/B♭ (Dm/E) Fm/E♭ (C) E♭
(Last time Fine)

By your hand, you feed your people

Susan Briehl,
based on Wisdom 16:20-21.26; 17.1a

CAMROSE
Marty Haugen

Refrain
Christ's own body, blessed and broken, Cup o'er flowing, life out-
(F#) A/C♯ (Bm) Dm (D7) F7/C (C/G) E♭/B♭ (G) B♭ (D/F♯) F/A (Em/A) Gm7 (D/F♯) F/A (G) G7/B
poured, given as a living token of your world redeemed, restored.
D.S.
(Asus4) Csus4 (A) C (D/F♯) F/A (D7) F7 (C/G) E♭/B♭ (G) B♭ (D/F♯) F/A (Dm7) Gm7 (D/F♯) F/C C7 (G/D) B♭/F (D) F
To optional interlude
D.S.
Optional Interlude
(G/D) B♭/F (D) F (Em7) Gm7 (D/F♯) F/A (Gmaj7) B♭maj7 (Em7/A) Gm7/C (A) C
D.S.

Let us see your face (Psalm 80)

Marty Haugen

Verses
1. Shep-herd of Is - rael, hear us, shine forth from your heav'n – ly throne;
2. God of the hea-vens, hear-ken, how long will your an - ger last?
3. Tears are the bread you give us, and tears are our bit - ter drink.
4. We are the vine you plan-ted, From E - gypt you brought us forth;
5. Turn now and see your peo - ple, be - hold us, O God of might;
(Em7) Gm7
(F) A♭
(Am7) Cm7
(Dm7) Fm7
Sop.
Stir up your strength and come to save us.
An - swer the fer - vent prayers we of - fer.
See how our foes re - vile and mock us.
Nur-tured us gen - tly as your peo - ple.
Care for this vine that you have plan-ted.
Alto
Stir up your strength and save us.
An - swer the prayers we of - fer.
See how our foes re - vile us.
Nur - tured us as your peo - ple.
Care for this vine you plan - ted.
poco rit.
(Am) Cm
(Em/G) Gm/B♭
(F) A♭
(C/E) E♭/G
(Dm7) Fm7
(F/G) A♭/B♭
(G7) B♭7

Be merciful, O Lord (Psalm 51)

Marty Haugen

* *The refrain may be sung in canon, with the second voice entering at 2, and the concluding bars as noted.*

 Octavo no: G-5644 (CSJ)

Verses
1. Have mer - cy on me, God, in your kind - ness. In your com - pas-sion blot out my of - fence. O wash me more and more from my guilt, and cleanse me from all of my sin.
2. For sure - ly I know my of - fen - ces; and my sin is e - ver be - fore me. Against you a - lone have I sinned; what is e - vil in your sight I have done.
3. A clean heart cre - ate for me, O God, put a stead - fast spi - rit with - in me. O cast me not a - way from your pre - sence, and take not your spi - rit from me.
4. Give back to me the joy of your sal - va - tion; and sus - tain me with a wil - ling Spi - rit. O Lord, o - pen my lips and my mouth shall de - clare your praise.
D/A
Am add9
Fmaj7
Dm7
Esus4
E
Am
Am/C
E
Dm/F
Bm7
Esus4
E

The Song and the Silence

Marty Haugen

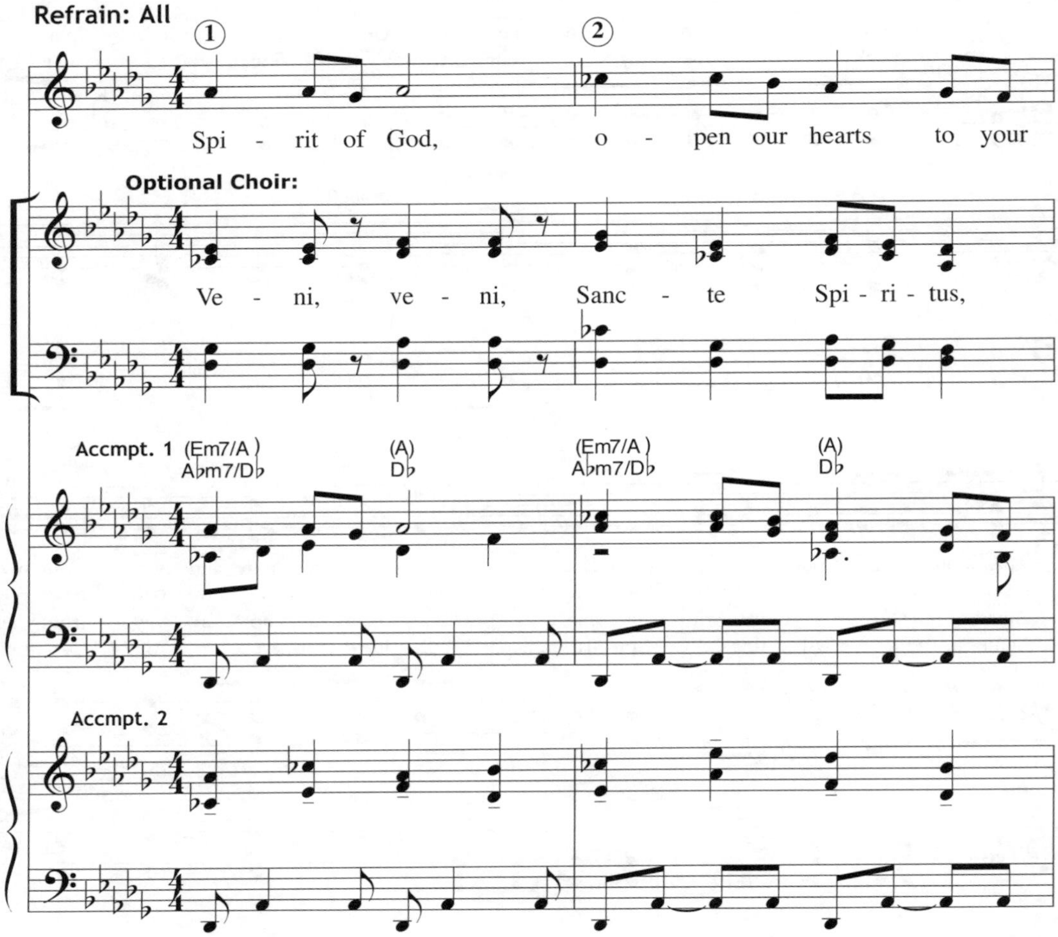

Refrain: All

① ②

Spi - rit of God, o - pen our hearts to your

Optional Choir:

Ve - ni, ve - ni, Sanc - te Spi - ri - tus,

Accmpt. 1 (Em7/A) A♭m7/D♭ (A) D♭ (Em7/A) A♭m7/D♭ (A) D♭

Accmpt. 2

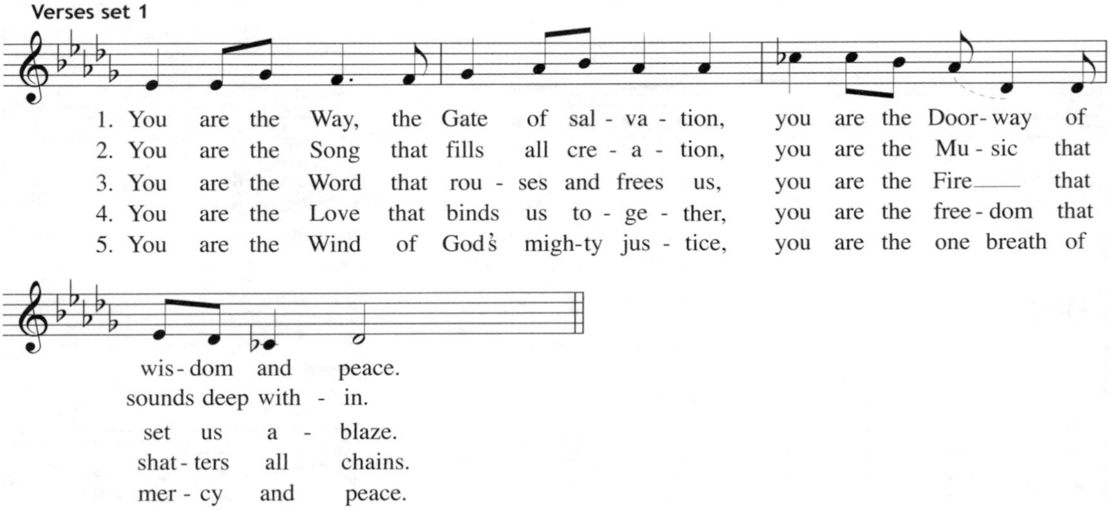

Verses set 1

1. You are the Way, the Gate of sal - va - tion, you are the Door-way of
2. You are the Song that fills all cre - a - tion, you are the Mu - sic that
3. You are the Word that rou - ses and frees us, you are the Fire___ that
4. You are the Love that binds us to - ge - ther, you are the free - dom that
5. You are the Wind of God's migh-ty jus - tice, you are the one breath of

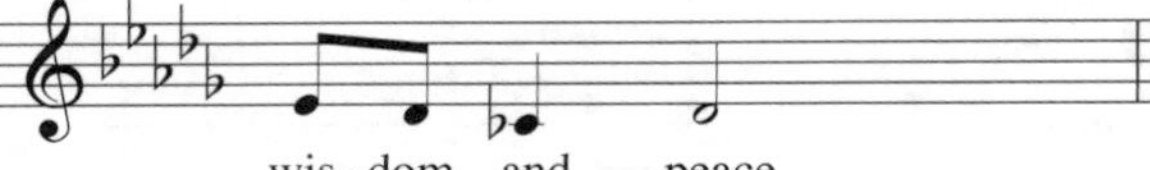

wis - dom and peace.
sounds deep with - in.
set us a - blaze.
shat - ters all chains.
mer - cy and peace.

3 4

song and your si - lence, dark-ness and light.

Sanc - te Spi - ri - tus, ve - ni.

Verses set 2

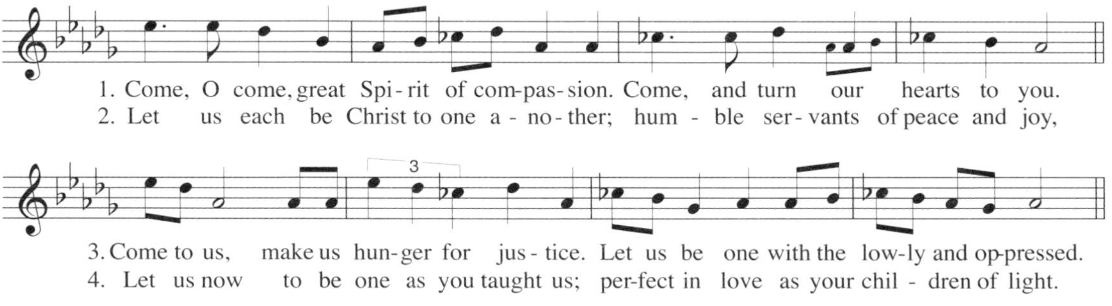

1. Come, O come, great Spi-rit of com-pas-sion. Come, and turn our hearts to you.
2. Let us each be Christ to one a - no-ther; hum - ble ser-vants of peace and joy,

3

3. Come to us, make us hun-ger for jus - tice. Let us be one with the low-ly and op-pressed.
4. Let us now to be one as you taught us; per-fect in love as your chil - dren of light.

Verses set 3

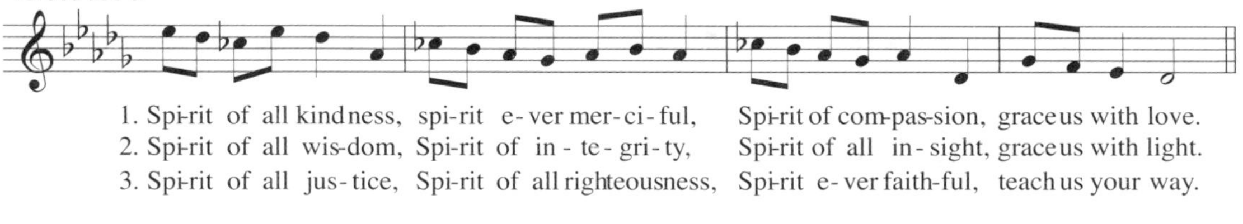

1. Spi-rit of all kind-ness, spi-rit e-ver mer-ci-ful, Spi-rit of com-pas-sion, grace us with love.
2. Spi-rit of all wis-dom, Spi-rit of in - te - gri-ty, Spi-rit of all in-sight, grace us with light.
3. Spi-rit of all jus-tice, Spi-rit of all righteousness, Spi-rit e-ver faith-ful, teach us your way.

Pilgrim's Song

Psalm 121

Marty Haugen

Verse 1
God will not let your foot be moved. God who keeps you will not
G G/B D D/F♯ G
slum - ber, The One who keeps Is - ra - el never slum - bers, ne-ver sleeps.
D/A A Bm G D Bm7 G Asus4 A
Verse 2
God will be the one who keeps you as a shade at your right hand. So the
D G/D D
sun shall not strike you by day, nor the moon in the night.
A/C♯ G/B D/F♯ Gmaj7 Asus4 A

Verse 3 *may be sung a capella*

God will keep you from all e - vil. God will al - ways guard your

D G/D D A/C♯ G/B A/C♯

life, guard your co - mings and your go - ings, from now and e - ver - more.

D F♯m7 Bm7 Em7 G/B Asus4 A

The Lord is my light

Psalm 27

Marty Haugen

Verses 1-3
1. When the wic - ked shall come to de - vour me, it is they who
2. There is one thing I ak of the Lord, there is on - ly
3. God will hide me in safe - ty and shel - ter in the day when
D Bm Gm/B♭ Gm6 F♯m7
stum - ble and fall. Though an ar - my en - camp all a -
one thing I seek: to dwell in the house of my
trou - ble is near. In the tent of my Gopd I take
Bm7 Em7 A Bm F♯m/A
3
bout me, though the bat - tle rage, I will not fear.
God all the days that I shall live.
re - fuge. God will set me high u - pon a rock.
Gm Gm/B♭ D/A G G/B Em/A A
D.C.

Verse 4
good - ness of the Lord,
I be - lieve I shall see the good of the Lord, in the
good - ness
good of the Lord,
D7 G/D Gm/D D A/C♯ G/B
Unison
land of the li - ving. Oh wait for the Lord, be
G A7 D G Gm/B♭ D/A
rit. D.C.
strong and take cou-rage, oh wait for the Lord.
rit.
G Gm/B♭ D/A G G/B A/C♯ let ring

Neither Death nor Life

Romans 8:11-19.22-25.28-35.38

Marty Haugen

all of cre - a-tion can e - ver se - pa-rate us from the
(G/B) B♭/D
(Adim7/C) Cdim7/E♭
(G/D) B♭/F
(Am7/D) Cm7/F
(G/D) B♭/F
Last time to CODA
our Lord.
To verses
love of God poured out in Christ Je - sus, Christ Je - sus our Lord.
(Am7/D) Cm7/F
G/D) B♭/F
(C/D) E♭/F
(D7) F7
(C/G) E♭/B♭
(G) B♭
Finish here if coda is not sung
Verses 1-3
1. Dwell in the One who raised Christ from the dead; though your
2. All who are led by the Spir - it shall live as
3. All of the suf - f'ring we now must en - dure is
(D) F
(D/F♯) F/A
(C) E♭
(G) B♭

bo - dy shall die, in Christ you shall rise through the
chil - dren of God, and heirs with Christ Je - sus, God's a -
noth - ing to the glo - ry so soon to be ree - vealed when cre -
(C) E♭
(G/B) B♭/D
(Am7) Cm7
(G/B) B♭/D
D.S.
Spi - rit who brings you to life.
dopt - ed and cho - sen and loved.
a - tion it - self is set free.
(C) E♭
(A7/C♯) C7/E
(C/D) E♭/F
(D) F
D.S.
Verses 4-6
4. All of cre - a - tion a - waits the new birth, the
5. All things work for good for the ones who love God, and if
6. Who can sep - a - rate us from the love of Christ? Will

full-ness of re-demp-tion, through la-bour pains of love, and
God is for us, then who can be a-gainst us? God's
hard-ship or dis-tress, per-se-cu-tion or fam-ine, or
so we wait in pa-tience and hope.
jus-ti-fied can-not be con-demned.
na-ked-ness or per-il or sword?
Coda
Christ Je-sus our
Unis.
Je-sus, Christ Je-sus, our Lord, poured out in Christ
Unis.
(C/D) E♭/F (D) F (B7) D7/F (Em7) Gm7 (A7) C7 (G/D) B♭/F
(G/B)(D7) B♭/F F7 (G) B♭ (G/B) B♭/D (C) E♭ (Cm/E♭) E♭m/G♭ (G) B♭
Je-sus, our Lord.
rit.

Bread of life from heaven

Based on John 6
Text by Susan Briehl

SANTO, SANTO Melody from Argentina
Adapted with new music by Marty Haugen

 Octavo no: G-5652 (GG)

Verses

1. Break now the bread of Christ's sac - ri - fice; Giv - ing
2. Seek not the food that will pass a - way; Set your
3. Love as the One who, in love for you, gave him
4. Take in the light that will nev - er dim, Taste the
5. Dwell in the One who now dwells in you; Make your
6. Drink of this cup and de - clare his death; Eat this
G G7/B C C/E
thanks, hun-gry ones gath - er round. Eat all of you, and be
hearts on the food that en - dures. Come, learn the true and the
self for the life of the world. Live in the One who is
life that is strong - er than death. Live in the One who will
home in the life - giv - ing Word. Know on - ly Christ, Ho - ly
bread and be - lieve Eas - ter morn. Trust his re - turn and, with
F F/A G/B C Bm7 E7
sat - is - fied; in Christ's pres - ence the loaves will a - bound.
liv - ing way, that the full - ness of life may be yours.
food for you, that your hun - ger and thirst be no more.
come, and then raise you up at the last with the blest.
One of God, and be - lieve in the truth you have heard.
ev - ry breath praise the One in whom you are re - born.
Am Am7/G D/F♯ D7 Gsus4 G7
D.S.
D.S.

Where your treasure is

Based on Luke 12:22-34

Marty Haugen

To verses
me. Where your trea sure is, your heart shall be.
(Em) Fm
(Em7/D) Fm7/E♭
(C) D♭
(C/D) D♭/E♭
(D7) E♭7
(C/G) D♭/A♭
(G) A♭
Last time
Unis.
trea-sure is, your heart shall be, where your treasure is, your heart shall
Unis.
(C) D♭
(C/D) D♭/E♭
(B7) C7/E
(Em7/D) Fm7/E♭
(C) D♭
(C/D) D♭/E♭
(D7) E♭7
fine
be.
(G) A♭
(C/G) D♭/A♭
(G) A♭
(Cm/G) D♭m/A♭
(G) A♭

Verses 1-3
(D/F♯) E♭/G
(D7) E♭7
(C/G) (G) D♭/A♭ A♭
1. What do you gain from all your wor - ry, What you should eat or what to wear?
2. Look at the ra - vens high a - bove you, They do not work their whole life through,
3. Be - hold the li - lies in their splen - dour, in grace and beau - ty are they dressed,
(B) C
(B7/D♯) C7/E
There is no peace in stress and hur - ry,
And yet God feeds them and pro - tects them,
And yet so soon their bloom is fa - ded.
(Em) Fm
(Em7/D) Fm7/E♭
(A/C♯) B♭/D
(A7) B♭7
(C/D) D♭/E♭
(D) E♭
D.S.
Do you not know that you are held with - in God care?
So how much more will God pro - tect and care for you?
So how much more will those who look to God be blessed?

Coda
(Em)
Fm
(B/D♯)
C/E
(G 6/D)
A♭6/E♭
Do not fear, lit-tle flock, for God de-lights to give you the
(A/C♯)
B♭/D
(Am7)
B♭m7
bles-sed reign of God. Give your pos-ses-sions to the
(G/B)
A♭/C
(F/C)
G♭/D♭
(C)
D♭
(C/D)
D♭/E♭
(D)
E♭
D.S.
nee-dy; gain a trea-sure that will not fade.

Only you, O God

Susan Briehl

BALM IN GILEAD, spiritual, arr. Marty Haugen

By the rivers of Babylon

Psalm 137

Marty Haugen

we sat down and wept as we re-mem-bered Zi - on, our home so far a - way.
we sat down and wept as we re-mem-bered Zi - on, our home so far a - way.
B♭/D
C/D
D(open)
C/D
B♭
C
D(open)
Verses
1. And there we hung our harps u - pon the wil - low trees as our
2. If ev - er I for - get you, O Je - ru - sa - lem, let this
3. Re- mem - ber, Lord, the ones who broke us, brought us low; Lord, re -
Harmony (verse 3)
Ooh
Gm
Dm
cap - tors laughed and called for joy - ful songs; For us there is no
hand once raised in praise to you go limp; And let my voice be
mem - ber those who raped and crushed our home; How hap - py they shall
Ooh
C/D
G/D
Am

Octavo no: G-6304 (TMH)

Once we sang and danced with gladness

Susan Briehl, vv. 1-2 based on Ps 137

KAS DZIEDAJA, Latvian melody arr. Marty Haugen

3. God, who came to dwell among us,
God, who suffered our disgrace,
from your own heart, grieved and wounded,
come the riches of your grace.

4. Come, O Christ, among these ashes,
come to wipe our tears away,
death destroy and sorrow banish;
now and always, come and stay.

Susan Briehl, based on Psalm 137

Turn my heart, O God

Marty Haugen

From all that leads to sin, to ho - li - ness and grace:
From sel - fish - ness and greed, to gene-rous, ca - ring love:
Give back to me the joy of wal - king in your way:
And let my spi - rit rest with - in your li - ving heart:
turn my heart, O God.
Come and
(C/E) (Dm) (C/G) (G7)
E♭/G Fm/A♭ E♭/B♭ B♭7
(C/G)
E♭/B♭
(Fm6)
Am6
From all des - pair and grief, to hope of life re - newed:
From all de - ceit and lies, to faith - ful - ness and truth:
O fill me with your grace that I might sing your praise:
For you a - lone can raise my wea - ry soul to life:
turn my heart, O God.
(C/E) (Dm) (C/G) (G7) (Am)
E♭/G Fm/A♭ E♭/B♭ B♭7 Cm
D.C.
Come and turn my heart, O God.
(Fm6)
A♭m6
(C/E) (C/G) (C/G) (G7) (C) (F) (G7)
E♭/G Fm/A♭ E♭/B♭ B♭7 E♭ A♭ B♭7
D.C.

Additional Verses
Psalm 51:1-9.10-17, adapted by MH
1. Have mer - cy, gra - cious God, for - give my sel - fish ways. O wash a - way my guilt and cleanse a - way my sin. I know my fai - lings well, they prey u - pon my mind.
2. I turned my face from you to seek out e - vil paths. Your pun - ish - ment is just, your sen - tence fair and right. You see me as I am: a sin - ner from my birth.
3. Great Lo - ver of all truth, teach wis - dom to my heart. O purge me, make me clean, and wash me new once more. Let songs of joy ring out from crushed and si - lent bones.
4. Cre - ate in me, O God, a clean and righ - teous heart. Do not a - ban - don me, but keep me close to you. Give back to me the joy of wal - king in your way.
5. Then I shall teach your path to bring the way - ward home. De - li - ver me from death that I might sing your praise. Ac - cept my gift to you: a bro - ken, con - trite heart.
D.C.

In Life and Death

Romans 6:3-11

Marty Haugen

To sung verses
Verses
Cantor
yours.
1. Just as Christ has been raised from the dead, so we might walk in the new-ness of life.
2. All the suff-'ring we now must en-dure, does not com-pare with the glo-ry to come.
3. So we live no lon-ger for our-selves, we live and die in the pro-mise of Christ.
(G/D) A♭/E♭ (D) E♭ (Bm) Cm (F#m/A) Gm/B♭ (Am7) B♭m7 (G) A♭
(Em7) Fm7 (D/F♯) E♭/G (G) A♭ (A) B♭
D.S.
Coda
yours.
rit.
(D) E♭ (Em7/D) Fm7/E♭ (Dmaj7) E♭maj7 (Em7/D) Fm7/E♭ (D) E♭

Watch, O Lord

From a prayer by St Augustine

Marty Haugen

Verses

18
Cantor
Assembly
Cantor, etc.
1. Tend your ai - ling ones:
2. Soothe your suffering ones:
3. Hold your grie-ving ones:
4. Guard your lit - tle ones:
in your love, Lord.
Rest your wea - ry ones:
Heal af - flic - ted ones:
Raise your fall - en ones:
Guide your searching ones:
in your
(G/B) B♭/D
(G/D) B♭/F
(D) F
(D7/F♯) F7/A
(C/G) E♭/B♭
(G) B♭
22
love, Lord.
Bless your dy - ing ones:
Shield your joy - ous ones:
Mend your bro - ken ones:
Grant us all your peace:
in your love, O Lord of all.
(D7/F♯) E♭/B♭
(D/F♯) F7/A
(Em) Gm
(Asus4) Csus4
(A) C

For God so loved the world

John 3:14-18 (R.v.16)

Marty Haugen

To verses
Final
much God loved the world, so much God loves the world. world.
Verse 1
(C) F
(D7/C) G7/F
(G/B) C/E
(F/A) B♭/D
(Em/B) Am/E
1. As Mo - ses lif - ted up the ser - pent, so that all who looked on it might
live, the Son of Man must be lif - ted up so that all who be lieve,
(Bb) E♭
(B♭/C) E♭/F
(F) B♭
(Am7) Dm7
all who look to him may have e - ter - nal life.
(Dsus4) Gsus4
(D) G
D.S.

Verse 2
2. God's Son came not to con-demn the world, but that the world may be
(C) F
(D7/C) G7/F
(G/B) C/E
(F/A) B♭/D
him, and all who be-lieve in the Son of God shall
saved through him, Ooh
(Em/B) Am/E
(C) F
(B♭) E♭
(B♭/C) E♭/F
(F/A) B♭/D
(F) B♭
D.S.
come to the light and live in the light and dwell in the heart of God.
(Am7) Dm7
(G/B) C/E
(C) F
(G/B) C/E
(Am7) Dm7
(Dsus4) Gsus4
(D) G

Salaam Aleikum
Traditional Ghanaian
Arranged by Marc Anderson and Marty Haugen
♩ = 74
Solo
Sa-laam a - lei - kum, sa-laam a - lei - kum,
Ho - yah! Ho -
sa-laam a - lei - kum,
1
sa-laam a - lei - kum.
yah! Ho - yah, ho-yah, ho-yah, ho-yah, ho - yah! Ho -
2
F
B♭
F
yah! Sa - laam a - lei-kum le, sa - laam a - lei-kum le, sa - laam a - lei-kum-
May peace be in your hearts, may peace be in your homes, may peace be in your
To repeat
D.S.
sa-laam a - lei - kum.
C7
To repeat
F
D.S.
le, sa - laam a - lei - kum le. le. Ho–
land, may peace be in our world. world.

Christ our peace

Words and music by Marty Haugen

Verses

Verses 1-5 Communion, Verses 6-7 General

Come, let us return

Hosea 6:1, 3, 6

Marty Haugen

Ostinato ending
Verses
bind you up.
1. Let us know, let us press on to know the Lord, for God's ap - pear - ing is as sure as the dawn.
2. God will come just as the faith - ful show - ers fall, just as the spring rains that wa - ter the earth.
3. God de - sires stead - fast love, not sac - ri - fice, know-ledge of God in - stead of of - fer - ings.
(Am/E Cm/G
(Em7) Gm7
(Am) Cm
(G7/F) B♭7/A♭
(Em7) Gm7
(Em7/G) Gm7/B♭
(Asus4) Csus4
(A7/G) C7/B♭
(F) A♭
(C/E) E♭/G
(Dm7) Fm7
(Am/E) Cm/G
(E7) G7
To Refrain

May we have the mind of Christ (Philippians 2:6-11)

Marty Haugen

 Octavo no: G-6854, *Two Simple Songs for Lent* (OYG)

Verses
1. Though he was in the form of God, he emp - tied him - self, ta - king on the form of a slave.
2. And, one like us in hu - man form, he hum - bled him - self, o - be - dient un - to death on a cross.
3. There-fore our God has raised him high, and gi - ven to him the name that is a - bove ev - ery name.
(C) E♭
(D7/C) F7/E♭
(G/B) B♭/D
(Am7) Cm7
To Refrain
(Em/G) Gm/B♭
(F#m7(b5)) Am7(♭5)
(Bsus4) Dsus4
(B) D
Coda
death u - pon a cross.
(F#m7(b5)) Am7(♭5)
(B) D
(Em) Gm
G E♭
(Am7) Cm7
(F#m7) Am7
(Bsus4) Dsus4
(B) D
(Esus4) Gsus4
(Em) Gm

For God, my soul waits in silence (Psalm 62)

*The first refrain may be sung by a soloist and repeated by all in unison; vocal harmonies may be added after the verses. The refrain and verses may alternate, or they may be sung simultaneously by treating the refrain as an ostinato or layering the verses (sung by a soloist or section of the choir) over the refrain (hummed or sung with words.)

Sheltered in the arms of God (Psalm 91)

Marty Haugen

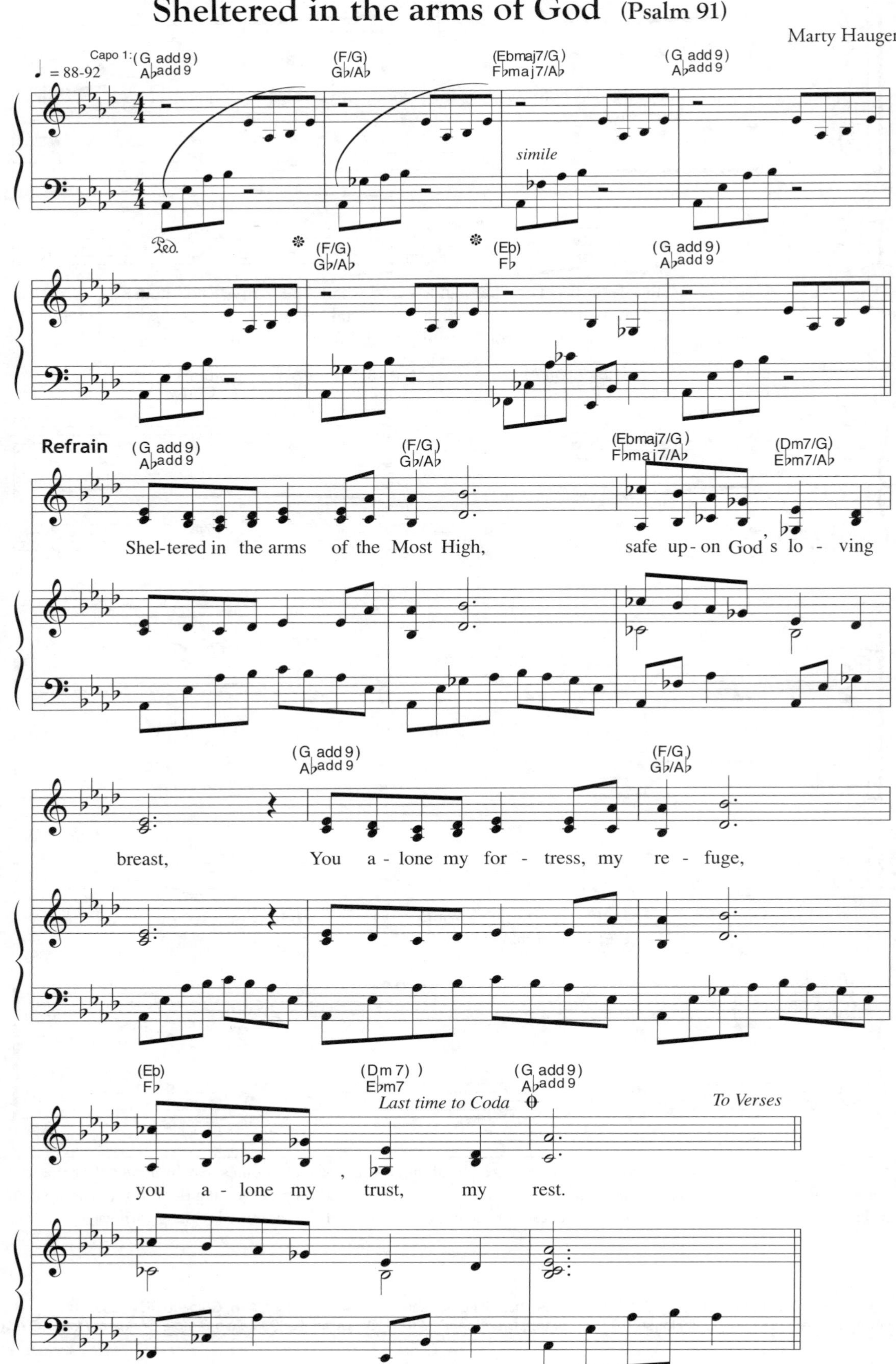

 Octavo no: G-6854, *Two Simple Songs of Hope* (OYG)

Love is flowing

Words and music by Marty Haugen

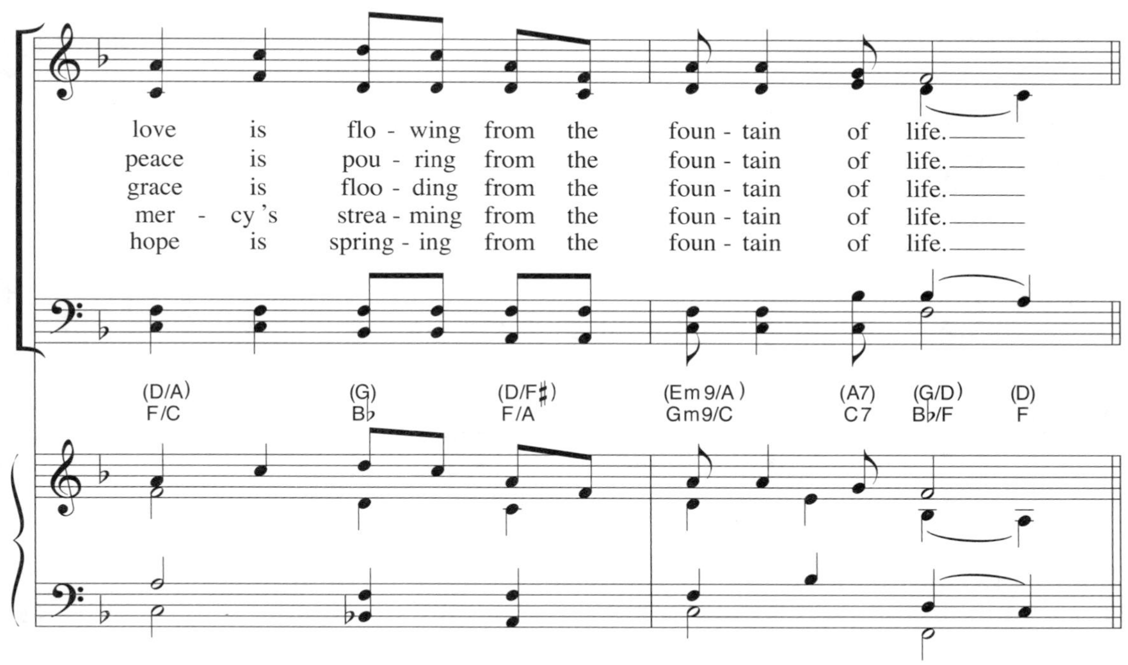

 Octavo no: G-6854, *Two Simple Songs of Gathering* (OYG)

God is with you

Isaiah 43:1b-2.5-7.18-19

Marty Haugen

* cue size notes: verses 4-6

(F) A (Am) C♯m (Dm 7) F♯m7 (C/G) E/B (G) B (F) A (Dm) F♯m (Dm7/C) F♯m7/E
be with you, they shall not o - ver- whelm you; when you walk through
east and west, from the north and the south – all God's sons and
ends of earth let the peo - ples as - sem - ble; you shall hear and
formed and made to be signs of God's glo - ry; God will draw you
things of old. I am ma - king a new thing; now it springs forth.
wil - der - ness, streams of life through the de - sert– li - ving wa - ter
8vb
(B♭) D (F/A) A/C♯ (B m7/E) E♭m7/A♭ (E) A♭
To Refrain
fire you shall not be burned.
daugh - ters from the ends of earth.
know the Word of God is true.
in and o - pen eyes and ears.
O - pen up your eyes and see.
nou - rish - ing God's cho - sen ones.
Coda
(Bm7) E♭m7 (D) G♭ (A/E) D♭/A♭ (Fdim7) Adim7 (G♭m) B♭m (G♭m7) B♭m7 (B) E♭ D♭ E♭7 (Bm7) E♭m7 (D) G♭ (A/E) D♭/A♭ (E7) A♭7 (A) D♭
pre - cious in God's sight. you are pre - cious in God's sight.

Send forth your Spirit

Psalm 103

Marty Haugen

♩ = 76

Refrain

Send forth your spirit, O God, send forth your spirit, O God, and re-

Verses

1. Bless the Lord, O my soul. O God, you are great indeed! You are
(2. You spread the) heavens out like a tent, you set your palace on the waters above. You have
(3. You have) fixed the earth on its foundation, and the seas that clothe is like a garment. At the
(4. You make) springs break forth in the valleys, giving drink to the beasts of the field, birds that
(5. You give) plants for the life of your creatures, food for strength, wine for joy, oil for gladness; mighty
(6. You have) made the moon to mark the seasons, told the sun when to rise and when to set. You make

Capo 1: (C) D♭ (F/C) G♭/D♭ (G7/C) A♭7/D♭ (C) D♭ (F/C) G♭/D♭ (G7/C) A♭7/D♭ (G/C) A♭/D♭

 Octavo no: G-6939 (OYG)

new the earth, re - new the earth, send
clothed in ma - jes - ty and splen - dour, and a -
fash - ioned the clouds as your cha - ri - ot and you
sound of your voice they rush and tum - ble; you have
sing from the trees by li - ving wa - ters, rains from
trees, the ce - dars of Le - ba - non, where the
night for the crea - tures of the fo - rest, they seek
(C) D♭ (F/C) G♭/D♭ (G7/C) A♭7/D♭ (C) D♭ (F/C) G♭/D♭ (G7/B) A♭7/C
forth your spi - rit, O Lord. Send
1
dorned in a robe of light.
ride up - on the wings of the wind. 2. You spread the
marked the bound - 'ries of their breadth. 3. You have
heav - en height that nou - rish the earth. 4. You make
birds and storks shall make their home. 5. You give
food from the hand of their God. 6. You have
(C) D♭ (F/C) G♭/D♭ (G7/C) A♭7/D♭ (C) D♭ (F/C) G♭/D♭ (G7/C) A♭7/D♭
Ostinato Accompaniment for Canon
(C) D♭ (F) G♭ (G) A♭ (C) D♭ (F) G♭ (G) A♭

Sing praise to God

Based on Psalm 146

Marty Haugen

 Octavo no: G-7597 (CBN)

not in hu - man might. Sing praise to God, our
formed the bound - less sea. Sing praise to God, whose
gives the hun - gry food. Sing praise to God, who
rai - ses those bowed low. Sing praise to God, who
loves the righ - teous one. Sing praise to God, in
A7/C♯ Dsus4 D C/D G Am7/G G
help and our sal - va - tion, Sing praise to God, our
pro - mi - ses are faith - ful. Sing praise to God, who
heals all your af - flic - tions. Sing praise to God, who
holds the wi - dow, or - phan. Sing praise to God, as
ev - ry ge - ne - ra - tion. Sing praise to God, O
G7 C A7/C♯ G/D B7/D♯ Em
hope and our de - light.
sets the pris - 'ner free.
grants us ev - 'ry good.
long as you shall live.
praise the Ho - ly One.
Am7 C/D C C/G G Am7/D Cm6/G G

Tell the Gospel's boundless riches

Delores Dufner, O.S.B. — Marty Haugen

2. See the Lord of God in Jesus,
caring for the poor oppressed,
calling out to weary pilgrims,
'Come to me and find your rest.'
See the love revealed by Jesus,
who with gentle, humble heart,
heart of God's immense compassion,
heart both human and divine.

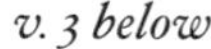
v. 3 below

4. Live the new commandment given:
'As I did, so you must do:
wash the feed of one another,
loving all as I love you.'
Live the love of Christ among us,
feeding, healing, setting free,
seeking out and bringing others
into love's community.

Verse 3 (SATB)

3. Praise the heart of God in Je - sus, self - less to his fi - nal breath,
gi - ving for our life his bo - dy, lo - ving e - ven un - to death.
Praise the sa - cred heart of Je - sus, ten - der love most tel - ling sign,
heart of God's im - mense com - pas - sion, heart both hu - man and di - vine.

One in the heart of Christ

1 Cor 11:23-26; John 17:21

Marty Haugen

Moderato ♩ = 84

D G6/D D Em7

Verses

1. On the night he was be - trayed, Je - sus blessed and broke the bread; he gave it to his friends and
2. On the night he was be - trayed, Je - sus blessed and shared a cup; he gave it to his friends and
3. On the night he was be - trayed, Je - sus prayed for those he loved, that all who served him might be
4. As we ga - ther in this place, hear the Word and break the bread, may we be - come what we re -

D/F♯ G G/B A D

G6/D Gm6/D D Em7 D/F♯ G G/B

said, 'This is my bo - dy, gi - ven for you; Share this in
said, 'This is my life - blood, gi - ven for you. Share this in
one: One in the Spi - rit, one in their love, one in the
ceive: God's li - ving Bo - dy, sent out to serve, one in the
A A7/G D/F♯ F C/E Em7 D/F♯
Refrain
When we eat this bread,
me - mo - ry of me.'
me - mo - ry of me.'
sa - cred heart of Christ.
sa - cred heart of Christ.
When we eat, when we eat this
Em7/G Em7 A/C♯ A D/F♯ G Em7 A7 F♯m7
bread, when we share this ho - ly cup, we pro - claim the
B7 Em7 F♯7 B7sus4 B7 G

Last time to Coda
death of Je - sus and ce - le - brate his pre - sence here.
D/F♯ Bm7 D/E G/A A7 D G A7
Coda (may also begin at *)
and ce - le - brate his pre - sence here, and ce - le -
Unis.
Bm7 Em7 G F♯7 Bm Gmaj7
brate his pre - sence here.
Em7 G/A A7 D G Gm/D D

Scriptural Index

Index of Named Tunes

Collections of Music by Marty Haugen

and guide to abbrevations

I send my light G-2635 (1978)
With open hands G-2636 (1980) WOH
Burn Bright (1980) G-2665 (separate octavo)
Gather us in G-2606 (1983) GUI
Psalms for the Church Year G-2664 (1983) *with David Haas* PsChY1
Mass of Creation G-2777, G-2768 (1984-5)
Mass of Creation Lutheran setting G-3823
Song of God among us G-2916 (1986) SGAU
Shepherd me, O God G-3107 (1987) SMG
Mass of Remembrance G-3480
Night of Silence G-3138 (1987) NOS
Psalms for the Church Year Vol. II G-3261 (1988) PsChY2
Tales of Wonder G-3320 (1989) TOW
Eucharistic Prayer for Children II: Mass of Creation setting G-3388
Holden Evening Prayer G-3460 (1990) HEP
Now the feast and celebration G-3488 (1990)
Wondrous Love G-3536 (1991) WL
World Peace Prayer G-3627 (separate octavo)
Welcome the child G-3802 (1992) WC
Agape: G-3959 (1993) AG
All are welcome G-4274 (1994) AW
The Song of Mark G-4416FS (1996) SM
The Church Gathers G-4560 (1996) *with Gary Daigle*
Up from the waters G-4835 (1997) UW
In the morning I will sing (Morning Prayer) G-4493
Come, let us sing for joy (a Lutheran Morning Prayer) G-4931
The Church Breaks Bread G-4960 1998 *with Gary Daigle*
The Song and the Silence G-5065 (1999) SS
Beneath the tree of life G-5220 (2000) BTL
Come let us sing for joy G-5235 (2001) CSJ
The feast of life G-5440FS (2000) TFL
Gift of God G-5690 (2002) GG
Turn my heart G-6277 (2004) T MH
Unfailing Light: an evening setting of Holy Communion G-6362K
That you may have life G-6614FS (2005) TYHL
That You May Have Life - A Liturgy for Lent G-6537; Years B and C G-7069
Only you, O God G-6941 (2007) OYG
In the days to come G-7079 (2007) IDC
Christ be near (with Tony Alonso, Michael Joncas) G-7581 (2009) CBN

Index of First Lines and Titles